D0953151

El Jefe

Also by Alan Feuer

Over There: From the Bronx to Baghdad

Still New York (with Ric Burns)

El Jefe

The Stalking of CHAPO GUZMÁN

Alan Feuer

FLATIRON
BOOKS

NEW YORK

EL JEFE. Copyright © 2020 by Alan Feuer. All rights reserved.
Printed in the United States of America. For information, address
Flatiron Books, 120 Broadway, New York, NY 10271.

www.flatironbooks.com

Designed by Steven Seighman

Library of Congress Cataloging-in-Publication Data

Names: Feuer, Alan, 1971– author.
Title: El Jefe : the stalking of Chapo Guzmán / Alan Feuer.
Description: First edition. | New York : Flatiron Books, 2020. |
Identifiers: LCCN 2020006743 | ISBN 9781250254504 (hardcover) |
    ISBN 9781250254528 (ebook)
Subjects: LCSH: Chapo, 1957– | Drug dealers—Mexico—Biography. |
    Drug control—Mexico.
Classification: LCC HV5805.C485 F47 2020 | DDC 364.1/3365092 [B]—dc23
LC record available at https://lccn.loc.gov/2020006743

Our books may be purchased in bulk for promotional, educational, or business
use. Please contact your local bookseller or the Macmillan Corporate and
Premium Sales Department at 1-800-221-7945, extension 5442, or by email at
MacmillanSpecialMarkets@macmillan.com.

First Edition: 2020

10 9 8 7 6 5 4 3 2 1

For JOANNA, who deserves it

Contents

Principal Characters

The Cops

STEPHEN MARSTON: Squad C-23, FBI, New York
ROBERT POTASH: Squad C-23, FBI, New York
RAY DONOVAN: Special Operations Division, DEA, Chantilly, Virginia
VICTOR VAZQUEZ: DEA, Mexico City field office
ANDREW HOGAN: DEA, Mexico City field office
BRIAN MAXWELL: technical operations, US Marshals Service, Mexico
JAKE HEALY: Homeland Security Investigations, Nogales, Arizona
FERNANDO CRUZ: DEA, Long Island field office
JUAN SANDOVAL: DEA task force, San Diego

The Cartel

JOAQUÍN "EL CHAPO" GUZMÁN LOERA: coleader, Sinaloa drug cartel
ISMAEL "EL MAYO" ZAMBADA: Guzmán's chief partner
DAMASO LÓPEZ NUÑEZ: Guzmán's chief of staff
ALEX CIFUENTES: Colombian drug lord, Guzmán's onetime personal secretary
JORGE MILTON CIFUENTES: Alex's older brother

CARLOS HOO "CONDOR" RAMÍREZ: Guzmán's bodyguard and personal secretary

MARIO LÓPEZ "EL PICUDO" OSORIO: Guzmán's Culiacán plaza boss

MARIO HIDALGO "EL NARIZ" ARGÜELLO: Guzmán's errand boy

LUCERO SÁNCHEZ: Guzmán's mistress

AGUSTINA ACOSTA: Guzmán's mistress

ANDREA VELEZ: Alex Cifuentes's personal assistant

JAVIER REY: Guzmán's biographer and screenwriter

IVÁN ARCHIVALDO GUZMÁN SALAZAR: Guzmán's son

JESÚS ALFREDO GUZMÁN SALAZAR: Guzmán's son

OVIDIO GUZMÁN LÓPEZ: Guzmán's son

JOAQUÍN GUZMÁN LÓPEZ: Guzmán's son

CHRISTIAN RODRIGUEZ: Guzmán's infotech consultant

CHARLY MARTÍNEZ: Guzmán's tech worker

IVAN "CHOLO IVAN" GASTELUM CRUZ: Guzmán's gunman and Los Mochis plaza boss

ARTURO AND ALFREDO BELTRAN-LEYVA: Guzmán's former friends, turned enemies

Joaquín was what he is and will be
A fugitive from justice
The lord of the mountain
And a boss in the city

—Los Canelos de Durango,
"The Lord of the Mountains"

ACT ONE

Server Jack

Nearly all crimes go unpunished in Mexico.

—*Field of Battle*, Sergio González Rodríguez

ONE

The Geek Squad Guy

June 2009–February 2010

It came in off the street one day—a tip, a lead, a rumor—whatever you cared to call it, it was one of the strangest things they had heard in their careers. Chapo Guzmán, the world-famous drug lord, had hired a young IT guy and the kid had built him a sophisticated system of high-end cell phones and secret servers, all of it ingeniously encrypted.

The unconfirmed report—perhaps that was the best way to describe it—had arrived that Friday in June 2009 when a tipster walked into the lobby of the FBI's field division office in New York. After his story had been vetted downstairs, it made its way up seven flights of stairs and landed with a curious thud among the crowded cubicles of C-23, the Latin American drug squad. For more than thirty years, the elite team of agents and their bosses had hunted some of the drug trade's biggest criminals, and while tall tales of their antics circulated constantly through its squad room near the courts in Lower Manhattan, no one in the unit knew what to make of this one. The tipster's account seemed credible enough but it was sorely lacking details: the only facts he had offered on the young technician were a first name—Christian—and that he was from Medellín, Colombia. All sorts of kooks spouting all sorts of nonsense showed up all the time at FBI facilities, claiming they had inside information on the Kennedy killing or knew someone who knew someone who knew where Jimmy Hoffa was. In what were still the early days of Internet telephony, it seemed a bit far-fetched that a twentysomething hacker had reached a deal with the world's most wanted fugitive and furnished him in hiding with a private form of Skype. As alluring as it sounded, it was just the sort of thing that would probably turn out to be a myth.

In the middle of a drug war, chasing myths was not enough to send C-23 into the field: reality was keeping the unit busy on its own. Three years after Mexico had launched a crusade against its brutal cartel kingpins, the country had erupted into incomparable violence, and much of the chaos had rolled downhill into American investigative files. Just that winter, a psychopath who called himself the Stewmaker had been caught near Tijuana after having boiled three hundred bodies down to renderings in caustic vats of acid. Two weeks later, a retired Mexican general was murdered in Cancún, his kneecaps shattered and his corpse propped up behind the steering wheel of a pickup truck abandoned on a highway. Since late 2006, the country's seven drug clans had all been at war with one another or the government—or sometimes both at once—and ten thousand people had already lost their lives. C-23 and other US law enforcement agencies pitched in when they could, opening cases and offering intelligence to their counterparts in Mexico. But in the past several months, conditions at the border had only gotten worse and had metastasized from an ordinary security emergency into something that resembled a full-scale insurrection. From the American point of view, the Sisyphean struggle to end the bloodshed—and to stem the flow of drugs heading north—seemed increasingly impossible despite the constant seizures, the federal indictments and the helicopter gunships sent as foreign aid.

In this target-rich environment, Chapo Guzmán was an interesting case. While he was neither the wealthiest nor the most sadistic trafficker in Mexico, he was by a matter of degree the most illustrious. His famous alias, "El Chapo"—often rendered "Shorty" but more accurately a reference to his squat, stocky frame—was globally familiar, with a recognition level that rivaled that of movie stars and presidents. Not since Pablo Escobar had ruled over Colombia had *la pista secreta*—the secret path of the narcotics business—seen a figure who was both a major criminal and a mass celebrity. For nearly twenty years, Guzmán had been at the center of the drug trade, involved in some of its best-known capers and disasters. In 1993, in his earliest brush with fame, he was sent to jail in Mexico for the murder of a Roman Catholic cardinal, Juan Jesús Posadas Ocampo, whose daylight killing at the Guadalajara airport introduced the world to the threat presented by Mexican cartels. Eight years later, in a move that earned him full folkloric status, Guzmán had escaped from prison, slipping out in a laundry cart after paying off his jailers.[1]

Ever since, he had been on the run, moving back and forth among a half-dozen hideouts deep in the Sierra Madre mountains, in the Mexican state of Sinaloa. Though he lived like an outlaw, he was treated like a king—loved by some, feared by many and inarguably one of the

1. The murder of Cardinal Ocampo, on May 24, 1993, was a seminal moment in Mexico, awakening the public to the rising power and violence of the country's drug mafias. It was also a seminal moment for Guzmán. He has always denied involvement in the killing; indeed, the evidence suggests that he may have been its target, not its perpetrator. Ocampo was likely killed, in accidental crossfire, when hit men from the Tijuana cartel tried to murder Guzmán. Guzmán never forgot that the cartel's leaders, the Arellano-Félix brothers, attempted to assassinate him or that they let him take the blame for Ocampo's death. The rancor spawned a bloody war between Guzmán and the brothers that raged intermittently from the early 1990s well into the first decade of the 2000s.

most powerful men in Mexico. A single word from him from one of his mountain dens could set in motion tractor-trailers in Nogales, planes in Cartagena and merchant freighters in Colón. At fifty-two—an improbable age in an industry that did not promote longevity—Guzmán had reached the height of his career, running his business freely and warring against his rivals, all while playing cat and mouse with those among the Mexican authorities who weren't on his payroll. While the American government was after him as well, a contrarian consensus had emerged in parts of Washington that at least he was contained in the Sierras, where he was spending exorbitant sums on his security and could not engage in the same bloody havoc that emergent mafias, like the Zetas or La Familia Michoacán, had recently been wreaking in the lowlands. It was also the case that no one—not the FBI, the DEA, nor their cousins in the intelligence community—had ever mounted a successful capture operation in the rugged region he had fled to. In the past two years alone, a panoply of American agencies had helped arrest Otto Herrera, Guzmán's connection to Colombia's cartels; Juan Carlos Ramírez, one of his top suppliers; and Jesus "El Rey" Zambada, the brother of "El Mayo" Zambada, his most important partner. The heir to Guzmán's throne—Mayo's son, Vicente—was in jail in Mexico City, and Pedro and Margarito Flores, the twin brothers who had handled much of his American distribution, were about to start recording him for US drug officials. By mid-2009, Guzmán himself was already under indictment in San Diego and Tucson and would soon face further charges in Brooklyn and Chicago. But after all of this—countless hours of investigative and prosecutorial effort—he had never spent a single day in an American court of law.

That was why C-23's new lead couldn't be discounted, as crazy as it sounded. The possibilities it promised were simply too enticing. It stood to reason that a man in Guzmán's position—on the lam, with far-flung operatives around the globe—would at least want a means of sending and receiving secret messages. Imagine the windfall if the drug squad in New York could hack into the system.

That is, if it actually existed.

While many of his coworkers shrugged at the story of the mythic cell-phone system, treating it like a piece of science fiction, Special Agent Robert Potash raised his hand and volunteered to run the rumor down. As the rookie in the unit, he had little else to do. Potash had joined C-23 only the year before and while he was as eager as anyone to succeed, he was still finding his feet among his older, more seasoned peers. One of those anomalies who came to law enforcement late in life, Potash had attended the FBI's academy in Quantico just before his thirty-seventh birthday, the outside age for new recruits. For a federal agent, his background was unusual. Trained as a mechanical engineer, Potash had spent fifteen years of well-paid boredom in the private sector, designing robots and lasers before he realized that what he really wanted to do was put together criminal cases, not expensive widgets. The son of a toolmaker from Connecticut, he had always been something of a tinkerer. Even approaching forty, he often still thought about himself as the handy little kid who built the neighborhood treehouse every summer and spent all winter working on a soapbox car in his garage.

Potash had never handled a cartel case before, but knowing of his technical bent, his bosses at C-23 had invited him to sit in on the interview with the tantalizing tipster. He left the conversation convinced there was something there and did not get much resistance from the squad when he stepped forward to investigate it further. Many of the unit's top agents didn't want the job, which, by the looks of it, was going to require studying encryption and reading up on arcane subjects like Voice over Internet Protocol. It was, to say the least, not the typical drug cop stuff of busting bad guys or grabbing kilos off the street. When you got down to it, it was more or less nerd work. But that was Potash's lane.

Joining him in his new assignment was his partner, Stephen Marston. Marston was eight times as experienced as Potash and nearly twice as tall. An agent cut from the classic mold—big, broad-shouldered, stolid, methodical—Marston, a New Yorker, had been at C-23 for much of the decade. In his own time in the unit, he had mostly focused on Colombians, among them the remnants of the co-caine cowboys from Medellín and Cali who had since the 1980s sup-plied cocaine to Mexican smugglers like Guzmán who worked along the border. While Marston didn't know much about technology—his computer degree from 1993 was obsolete—he did know quite a bit about investigating drug cartels. And something in the tipster's re-port had caught his eye.

Under questioning, the tipster had explained that shortly before the young technician Christian had gone to work for Guzmán, he had built a beta version of his system for another trafficking group, the Cifuentes family, one of Colombia's stealthiest and most success-ful smuggling organizations. Known as the "invisible clan" for their ability to work beneath the radar, the Cifuenteses were, like Chris-tian, based in Medellín. The family had a long and tangled history with Guzmán and had for years been shipping him their product in everything from King Commander turboprops to long-range shark and tuna boats. Marston knew that the tipster's story might have had a few implausible details, but he recognized its basic inner logic. If some of the Cifuenteses had acquired a new technology, it would cer-tainly be reasonable to think that they had passed it on, through the man who had developed it, to their longtime friend and ally.

Meticulous as always, Marston was not about to raise an alarm—or his boss's expectations—without first thoroughly confirming the ac-count. In the FBI, if you were smart, you always promised less than you delivered. As he and Potash started on the case, Marston decided that he needed proof of concept: some hard evidence that the secret system was more than just a pipe dream.

What he really needed, when he thought about it further, was one of the damned phones.

They started with their colleagues in Colombia.

After squeezing the tipster for all that he was worth, Marston and Potash decided to run his story past the experts on the ground: the FBI's legal attaché team and their DEA equivalents in Bogotá. They arranged a call with the embassy and to their surprise, when they mentioned Christian's name, everyone seemed to know who they were talking about. A young technician—Christian Rodriguez, they were told—ran a small business in Medellín repairing computers and setting up communications networks. Rodriguez was also known to dabble from time to time in the city's black-hat hacking scene. Though there wasn't much in the way of solid proof, the agents in Bogotá were confident it had to be their man.[2]

Signing off, Marston and Potash dwelled on their discovery: the young kid that Chapo Guzmán had brought in as his infotech consultant appeared to have a day job as Medellín's Geek Squad guy.[3]

Once they had his full name and birth date, it was pretty much a routine full-court press. Working with their counterparts in Bogotá, Marston and Potash put together a profile, running down and

---

2. Rodriguez is not the young man's real last name, but it has been used here at the request of federal officials.

3. The FBI has never fully explained why Christian Rodriguez was already on Bogotá's radar in mid-2009.

identifying anyone they could find with a connection to Rodriguez: family members, old friends, lovers, neighbors, acquaintances and colleagues. Medellín's tech world at the time wasn't like New York's or San Francisco's, with tens of thousands of salaried employees and large conglomerates lording it over a field of plucky start-ups. The scene down there was small and fragmented, largely based on consulting gigs and casual relationships. Some of those relationships, given the city's history with crime, seemed to straddle the line between legal commerce and far less sanctioned ways of making money. The agents in New York were looking for an in, someone who knew the young technician and might be persuaded to give them information. Within a month of developing their dossier, they settled on a target: another young man on the make, one who had done business with Rodriguez in the past. Flying down to Medellín to meet him that summer, they used their charms—and a quantity of taxpayer dollars—to convince him to cooperate.

The Associate, as they came to call this second source, pulled off a triumph by September: he scared up one of Rodriguez's encrypted phones. It was an E-series Nokia with a dark gray case, a color screen and a simple little keypad. Though it didn't look like much, Marston and Potash knew that it was top of the line. The E-71 was one of the earliest smartphones on the market, not exactly NASA-level tech, but not a flip phone either. And it wasn't cheap: When Marston and Potash googled the device, they found it was selling for seven hundred dollars, nearly twice as much as their government-issue BlackBerries. One thing was for certain: there weren't a whole lot of people walking around with an E-71 in the early fall of 2009.

The Associate was coy as to how he had procured the device. But Marston and Potash weren't too particular. They had what they were after and had come to learn that in a cocaine capital like Medellín, it was often the case that the objects people handled, like the gossip they provided, moved in mysterious ways. Things in Medellín could and did suddenly appear, sometimes without much explanation. Granted, of course, that the terms of the agreement—and the price—were right.[4]

Back stateside, they took their prize to the FBI's Engineering Research Facility in Virginia.

The giant complex—known as ERF—was where the bureau's best eggheads worked their magic: packet sniffing, passcode breaking, systems analysis and various other digital dark arts. The imposing structure on the agency's training grounds in Quantico all but quivered with the might and weight of the government. Pulling up outside, Marston and Potash were confident that the brains at ERF would take one look at Rodriguez's device and it would wither beneath their gaze, revealing all its secrets.

But as soon as they walked in, the techs approached them as though they were carrying a dirty bomb. Grabbing the phone from the agents' hands, they shoved it into a Faraday bag and quickly locked the seal. Potash was taken aback. Perhaps he should have realized that if they were trying to study Guzmán's phone, the phone might be trying to study them as well. In the end, that wasn't the case: the phone was dormant and not emitting signals. But it was instructive to have learned that the kingpin's little Nokia could send a

---

4. If the details of the Associate's identity seem sketchy, that's because the FBI has chosen to make them so. The bureau has never revealed its source's name, occupation or the nature of his relationship with Christian Rodriguez. Bureau officials describe the two men's ties in only the vaguest terms, saying that while the Associate had dealings with Rodriguez, he was not himself a techie. "He emerged from the soup of Medellín where everyone is always making moves," said one official with knowledge of the case. That, to say the least, is not an enlightening description, which is, of course, the point. The secrecy with which the FBI has handled the Associate and the speed with which its agents found both him and Christian Rodriguez smells faintly, yet distinctly, of the work of the intelligence community.

message to its master if it wanted: *Hey, boss, the* gringos *have me at a hacking lab in Quantico.*

That, however, was the only thing they learned that afternoon. After running through a suite of tests, the techs came back and said, "Sorry, guys, this one can't be cracked." Marston and Potash couldn't believe it. Even ERF, with all of its diagnostic firepower, wasn't able to get into the thing? It was, if nothing else, persuasive verification of Christian Rodriguez's tradecraft. Their proof of concept was looking more intriguing—and spookier—by the day.

They talked about it later, driving home.

The way the techs had explained it, there were several different overlapping problems. Among the most important was that Rodriguez's phone was using an early form of point-to-point encryption. Point-to-point encryption is a defensive technology that requires two codes: one code scrambles messages and prepares them for delivery; the second receives the messages and puts them back together. Without both codes, any communication captured as it passes in between two phones—law enforcement's typical means of interception—would come out looking like a bunch of garbled nonsense. Potash in particular understood that this type of encryption was the real deal, the gold standard of information security. It meant that Guzmán's Nokias could talk to one another completely in the dark.

The second problem was the underlying hardware. The bureau's techs had quickly determined that the E-71 wasn't running off of normal commercial infrastructure—a cellular service, for example, owned by a standard provider like AT&T or Verizon. It was instead running off the Internet on its own private server. And the server wasn't only private; it was funky and furtive and seemed to be forever moving around. Potash had been hoping that ERF could have tracked the system's IP address back to a tech firm in Colombia and told him that Rodriguez was managing his server operation on his lunch break from a secret little closet in the basement. If that had been case, it would have been easy. The FBI could prevail on the company to do the right thing; if the bosses didn't comply, agents could simply serve a warrant.

But there was no company and no secret closet.

When the techs at ERF dug into the server's address, it was fifteen shades of weird. They could see its identifying digits—number-dot-number—but they couldn't determine its location, which appeared to have been anonymized and was skipping across the globe. This sort of thing was not mainstream technology in 2009. It was far more sophisticated than anyone suspected.

Potash was as frustrated as he was impressed. You couldn't serve a warrant on an anonymous location. It was almost like a snitch had told him that a ton of pure cocaine was sitting in a warehouse somewhere ready for the taking, then handed him a battering ram to break through the door.

The problem was: Where was the door?

No one knew.

Whoever had built this thing, he thought, was a serious, MIT-level systems engineer. An engineer himself, Potash felt like a kindergartner holding it in his hands.

They became obsessed with the kid. They couldn't stop talking about him, thinking about him, trying to figure out what made him tick.

It was obvious to both of them that he was some sort of prodigy. And yet for a techie, Rodriguez had hardly left behind a digital trail. Aside from his ties to the Cifuentes family, he didn't seem to have much of a resumé or client list for them to follow either. The Associate helped fill in some details. In their conversations and frequent trips to see him, the Associate told the agents that Rodriguez wasn't a lawbreaker by nature; he was simply trying to hustle his way through a criminal economy in which some of the people who signed up for his services were not exactly what they claimed to be. Whatever he was, investigating the mystery of the young technician had started to develop the itch of an addiction. The agents' wives began to joke that they were spending more time with one another than with anyone else. When that joke aged, there was a new joke: When they threw their husbands out, the wives complained, Marston and Potash would no doubt find a place together and probably be happier working around the clock.

It didn't help that, by the end of the year, they decided that they needed to be on the ground in Colombia. In mid-December 2009, a few months into what the New York office was now calling Operation Server Jack, they booked a flight to Bogotá and flew down with a Power-Point of everything they knew about their case. Arriving at the embassy, they shook their colleagues' hands and set up shop. But when they flashed their slides of Guzmán, Christian and the secret system, it provoked the same confused looks that the initial tip had gotten in the squad room in New York. Everyone was interested, of course. Computers? *Cool.* But no one really got it. So wait a minute, Marston and Potash were asked, it's not a landline, but it's not a cell phone either? What the heck is it? How do they pay their monthly bill?

What the team in Bogotá wanted to discuss was drugs. And not just any drugs—specifically the drugs being sold by the Cifuentes organization. Marston and Potash weren't the only agents with hooks into the family; the DEA had been on to them for months. It was explained to the visitors that two investigations were currently underway in Miami and New York, the latter being fed by a wiretap that the Colombians were running with the US embassy's assistance. The tap, which had been in place for the past two years, was almost unimaginably vast. Hundreds of phones were being monitored, and in terms of raw numbers, the intercepts were already in the neighborhood of fifteen, sixteen thousand. Nearly every member of the sprawling clan—the matriarch, Carlina; her nine adult children; and God knew how many nieces and nephews—were under surveillance. The Cifuentes family could barely order Chinese food without the embassy knowing if they had gotten white rice or brown rice in the bag.

Which meant, of course, that the DEA guys liked to talk about the family—and did. Marston and Potash didn't mind. The history of the Cifuentes organization was horribly confusing, a dense web of shifting alliances and violent executions. But it was useful, if only to put Christian into context. It was interesting to learn that after starting out as small-time smugglers who trafficked cigarettes and whiskey through the port in Medellín, the family had clawed its way to power mainly by hedging bets and striking up strategic ties with most of Colombia's larger, stronger crime groups. Fernando Cifuentes, the oldest brother in the clan, had once served as a bodyguard for Efraín Hernández, a capo in the North Valley drug cartel. The second brother, Pacho, had gone to work for Pablo Escobar, serving as a pilot. After a stint in Mexico working with Mayo Zambada, Chapo Guzmán's partner, a third Cifuentes brother, Jorge Milton, had traveled to Texas and built a brisk business bringing coke into the state. Only Alex Cifuentes, the baby of the family, had failed to uphold its famous name. Plagued by addiction and aggression, Alex had bounced around for years working for his brothers in subordinate positions, all while drinking prodigiously and raising hell, beating up taxi drivers and setting fire to nightclubs. Even into his thirties, Alex had remained a kind of dilettante, happy to spend his family's fortune, but never quite able to hold a steady job.

It was in the early 2000s, Marston and Potash were told, that the Cifuenteses had embarked on their partnership with Guzmán. At the time, the kingpin was just beginning to rebuild his business after breaking out of prison in 2001. Pacho Cifuentes had by that point taken control of his family's own business after Fernando had been killed, and found himself in charge of an illegal empire cloaked by a series of quasi-licit holdings in real estate, cattle ranches, airlines, construction firms and emerald mines. Pacho and Guzmán, sensing an opportunity, came to an arrangement. Pacho agreed to fly cocaine from one of his private airstrips and a hangar at the Medellín airport into western Mexico on one of Guzmán's latest acquisitions: a small fleet of carbon-fiber airplanes that could, or so the kingpin said, pass through radar undetected. When the deal turned out to be a huge success, others soon followed and Pacho brought Jorge and Alex into Guzmán's orbit. It was a testament to how enmeshed they all became that within a few years their sister, Dolly, also started to work with Guzmán.

There was one last piece to the story, and it was directly relevant to the New York agents' case. In April 2007, Pacho had himself been killed. There had long been rumors that he was an American informant and, apparently believing they were true, Colombia's most feared cartel, the Oficina de Envigado, sent a hit team disguised as policemen to murder him at his ranch near Medellín. The assassination devastated the younger Cifuentes brothers—and not just for the usual reasons. After Pacho's death, Jorge and Alex discovered that he owed as much as ten million dollars to Guzmán and other top drug lords in the region. Now the leader of his family, Jorge flew to Mexico and reached his own arrangement with the kingpin. Fearing for his safety in Colombia, he announced he was moving down to Ecuador and proposed to pay off Pacho's debt by sending cocaine to Sinaloa from a series of the country's western seaports. In setting up the project, Jorge spared no expense. He conspired to have the drugs protected by a corrupt Ecuadorean army officer and bribed the navy for the latest information on prowling American ships. To further indemnify his scheme, Jorge made a personal gesture: He suggested sending Alex, who had just gotten sober, to live with Guzmán in the mountains as a kind of human collateral. Jorge's deal, with its insulating layers of insurance and corruption, appealed to the kingpin and he took it.

All this history finally closed the circle. Marston and Potash already knew by then how Christian Rodriguez had made his way to the Cifuentes family; now they understood how Jorge and Alex had made their way to Guzmán.

As the crash course came to an end, one of the DEA guys had a question. It concerned their own wiretap. There were moments on the wire, he said, when one Cifuentes would suddenly tell another, "Hey, let's continue this discussion on the Spark." The phrase itself was strange enough, but even stranger, it seemed to be used only when the intercepts were getting good and sensitive subjects were about to come up.

The DEA was working on a theory that the Spark was some sort of meeting place—a hideout or a soundproof chamber the family would retreat to for private conversations. But they didn't really know.

Marston and Potash knew—or at least, they had a guess. The Spark, they told their colleagues in Bogotá, was probably the forerunner to Guzmán's system that their tipster had mentioned: the beta version that Rodriguez had built for the Cifuentes clan.

You could all but see the investigative synapses firing in the room. The Cifuentes family had *two* communications systems. One of them, existing in the open light of day, the DEA had been monitoring for months. But the other system, secret like Guzmán's was, was hidden in the dark.

Poor bastards, Potash thought. It was a bit like living in a house for thirty years and then one morning discovering a door in the basement leading to a whole new house beneath it. He pitied them a little. If only because he recognized the feeling.

Once it had a name, the DEA wanted access to the Spark. But at least so far, the kingpin's similar system had stumped the finest minds the FBI had thrown at it. In the absence of a technical solution—and there didn't seem to be one yet—getting into either secret system was going to require getting to Rodriguez.

From the outset of Operation Server Jack, Marston and Potash had debated the idea of approaching the young Colombian. In one of their recent meetings with the Associate, their source had told them that even though Rodriguez was making loads of money, he was petrified on an almost daily basis to be working for Chapo Guzmán. While that made him susceptible to an approach, which was clearly an advantage, it also made him skittish, which was not. Talking it over with their bosses in New York, Marston and Potash decided that they needed to be careful: they would get only one chance to flip Rodriguez. If they made a play for him and the kid said no, Operation Server Jack was almost certainly over. In the best-case scenario, the young technician would simply disappear. But in the worst, he would shut the system down.

There was, however, another option—an undercover sting. When Marston and Potash came back from Colombia, they holed up in the squad room trying to game it out. The goal, of course, was leverage: to catch Rodriguez selling his technology to a criminal, preferably on camera. While the obvious choice was to run a "customer" against him posing as a member of a Mexican cartel, no one in the unit was persuaded that was viable. If Christian Rodriguez valued his life, even in the slightest, he would never offer his services to anyone who could be perceived as Guzmán's competition. An Italian undercover wasn't much better, they decided. Everyone agreed that the Mafia gambit was a bit played out.

Then it came to them. Marston had an old friend in the bureau's local Russian squad. A Russian might work; they weren't like Mexicans. A Russian organization wouldn't want to bring a techie deep into their business and lock him in with a long-term contract or a loyalty oath. Russians were independent. They would want to do things simply: buy a product at a reasonable price, learn how to use it, then run it by themselves.

When Marston called his friend, the friend said he knew someone who might be good for them: a real Russian gangster who was already in custody, working off the sentence of his own federal charge. If the Russian was as good as the friend was saying, they might be able to use the Associate to nudge Rodriguez into meeting him.

A few days later Marston and Potash went to meet their undercover. The Russian, they discovered, was a large, imposing man with a black leather jacket, a hard-core scowl and a heavy Slavic accent.

He was more than good. He was perfect.

TWO

Up in the Mountains

Christian Rodriguez would not have been surprised when he received a phone call from his countryman, Alex Cifuentes, as Christmas approached in late 2008. Rodriguez had, after all, just completed a special project for the well-known trafficker and two of his closest siblings. A few months earlier, Rodriguez had gone to visit Dolly Cifuentes, Alex's older sister, at her rose-filled home in Medellín to discuss the encrypted communications system that she and her brothers needed to conduct the more clandestine aspects of their business. Rodriguez, new to the job of serving criminals, came up with some ideas, and they were good enough ideas that Dolly suggested running them past her brother Jorge, who was down in Ecuador working on the family's latest venture. Rodriguez went to Ecuador, met with Jorge and after he returned presented his new clients with a handcrafted product: a firewalled cell-phone system that ran on its own private network and allowed its users to exchange protected texts.

Though Rodriguez had just turned twenty-one, he looked much

younger. He was, for one thing, conspicuously short—not much more than five feet four—and his wan skin, pudgy cheeks and little hacker's belly betrayed him as the kind of man who had spent his life in front of screens. Long drawn to the shadows of the digital world, Rodriguez had gone to school for systems engineering, but dropped out after only three semesters to launch a cybersecurity firm. The business, for the most part, was legitimate—Web design, tech support, network administration—though on occasion, to make ends meet, he did, admittedly, accept assignments from customers whose own work was somewhat less than lawful. It was the sort of thing that was, perhaps, bound to happen in a town like Medellín.

Alex Cifuentes had called that winter on behalf of such a customer: his own new employer, the kingpin Chapo Guzmán. In late 2007, Alex had been sent into the Sinaloan mountains by his older brother Jorge, and ever since he had been working as Guzmán's personal secretary, looking after almost every aspect of an expansive criminal empire. The task of serving as the right-hand man to a drug lord with a multibillion-dollar bottom line and employees everywhere from Chicago to the South China Sea could, at times, be maddening. One day, it might mean dealing with a lost load of coca paste; the next, attending to the purchase of a crate of RPGs. When Alex took the position—to secure his family's business with the kingpin—he was still recovering from a debilitating surgery brought on by the ravages of alcohol. Gastric fluids, leaking from his stomach, had turned into a fistula and resulted in a near fatal case of pancreatitis. In his weakened state, Alex was nonetheless placed in charge of paying Guzmán's gunmen, wrangling his pilots, managing his airstrips, overseeing his motor pool and supervising the kaleidoscopic churn of coke deals, pot deals and heroin deals that packed his busy schedule each day.

While the kingpin's nights in the mountains could often be a blur of mistresses and whiskey, the rush began at noon when he woke up to take his morning meal. There was a small shack near his cabin where two maids cooked him breakfast on an old gas stove. As soon as he sat to eat, Alex or a colleague would be called upon to deliver an intelligence report. Had the troops been active at their base that day? Were any of his enemies on the move? After the briefing came his list of daily messages: perhaps one of his sons had called, or his plaza boss in Mazatlán.[5] From his simple kitchen table, Guzmán would issue orders for a cash drop in Los Angeles or a checkup on production at his meth labs in Jalisco. Alex was expected to take down these instructions in a notepad. But it was only after the kingpin finished his meal that he began to work in earnest. Then he would pick up his favorite means of communication, a long-range cordless phone, and step outside beneath the high Sierra pines to return his calls while strolling under the trees.

When Alex first arrived in the mountains, Guzmán had been living there for the better part of a decade. Born in the Sierras, in the village of La Tuna, the kingpin knew firsthand the advantages they offered to a fugitive. The local roads, bent with rocky switchbacks, were perfect ambush country and were easy to defend against attack. Much of the rough terrain could be approached only by foot or on off-road vehicles and was more or less impassable to military convoys. Snaking south through Sonora, Sinaloa and Durango, the ancient Sierra Madres had always been a sanctuary for renegades, and the region's austere landscape of scrub and sky had produced a culture of wary insularity. In the small towns clinging to the hillsides, the resi-

---

5. The plaza is the basic geographic unit of the Mexican drug trade, the equivalent of what the Italian Mafia refers to as turf. Plazas are generally centered around major cities, though they often range into outlying areas. Cartel leaders can control many plazas; Guzmán held plazas in Culiacán, Mazatlán, Los Mochis, along the border and up and down the country's west coast. A kingpin's designated proxy in a plaza is known as a plaza boss. Plaza bosses are responsible for managing business and maintaining security in their regions. In exchange, they receive a cut of the plaza's profits.

dents were stubborn, independent and suspicious of the government. Time and experience had taught them not only to distrust the state, but to turn a blind eye to the dusty trucks of outlaws bouncing up the twisting mountain passes. Guzmán knew he could rely on the loyalty of their terror. With families of their own to protect, they would likely keep their mouths shut if they saw him, and might even tip him off to approaching troops or hide him in a basement if he found himself in need.

But after six years of hard and constant use, many of Guzmán's mountaintop retreats were in a state of disrepair—not that they had been much to begin with. Spartanly equipped with wood-plank huts, cheap plastic furniture and power systems running off of used car batteries, the rustic compounds had the temporary, makeshift look of logging camps. Blackened cookware hung from nails on the sides of moldy buildings, and perishable rations were left outside to rot. Guzmán's thirty-man security team—filthy, rowdy cells of former soldiers—slept on the floor in ramshackle barracks and were provisioned once a month by planeloads of bullets, beans and tortillas flown in from below. Some of the encampments had small, bucolic touches—fruit trees in the yard, dance *palapas*, Cornish hens—but they were mostly a disaster.

It was not at all what Alex Cifuentes, an art collector and a connoisseur of thousand-count sheets, had been accustomed to. Within a few months of taking his new job, he began to make improvements, bringing in refrigerators, washer-dryers and plasma-screen TVs. The Internet service in the mountains was particularly bad, generally running off of shoddy rooftop satellite antennae that often failed in the torrential monsoon rains that blew through every summer. For a man who was obsessed with technology, and often kept ten different sets of his cordless phones on hand, it was all but inconceivable that Guzmán had such a glaring gap in his communications system.

But Alex had decided to improve that too. Which is why he had called Christian Rodriguez.

It wasn't easy getting to the mountains. Most people made the trip by plane, taking off from an improvised runway in a cornfield on the outskirts of Culiacán, the Sinaloan capital. Culiacán was a bustling city of slightly less than seven hundred thousand not far from the Gulf of California, and was to the Mexican drug trade what the South Side of Chicago was to Al Capone. For Guzmán's organization, it served as both a business district and a stomping ground. Culiacán lay in close proximity to the busy ports in Mazatlán and Escuinapa; it was also a financial center of a sort with abundant private companies, some of which were used to launder money. On its streets was everything that a narco-trafficker needed: nightclubs, casinos, sports-car dealerships, designer boutiques, cobblers selling ostrich-skin boots and beauty salons that for a price would encrust a girlfriend's fingernails in diamonds.

The flight from Culiacán to Guzmán's mountain bases was only forty minutes, but those could be a harrowing forty minutes. The local winds were treacherous, and journeys needed to be scheduled for early in the morning or late in the afternoon when they were low. Even then, passengers were often forced to crowd into the kingpin's planes with loads of supplies—sacks of rice or giant coolers of seafood—and with all that extra cargo weight, the pilots found it difficult at times to maintain proper altitude. Arriving at the compounds could be equally precarious. One of the kingpin's airstrips was carved into a cow patch: when it was not in use, the cattle were herded back in place to disguise it from the sky. Another—far more perilous—was built in the shape of a ski slope. It was hazardously short, and inbound aircraft came in hard on the steep upward incline in order to slow down.

That was the runway Christian Rodriguez landed on just days after receiving Alex's call. The young technician had been terrified from more or less the moment he climbed aboard his plane, a rickety little Cessna that bounced around as it left the sprawl of Culiacán behind and passed above the highland peaks and valleys. Now, as he stepped out into a broad mountain clearing, he was greeted by the kingpin's usual welcome crew, which couldn't have been any more consoling. Gunmen dressed in camouflage rolled up to meet him in a fleet of muddy ATVs. One of the soldiers, strapped like the rest with an AK-47, threw Rodriguez on the back of his vehicle and took off up a rutted dirt road.

Terror was the commonest reaction to the mountains. The first time Jorge Cifuentes landed there in his own flimsy single-engine plane, he prayed aloud in panic. Another visitor, riding on the rough road from the airstrip, once saw a dead man hanging naked from a tree. A third was so unnerved by his stay in the Sierras that after flying back to Culiacán, he hurried into a church. Lighting two candles, he dropped down onto his knees. "In a trip like this," he later told a friend, "sometimes people don't come back."

Alex was waiting up in camp. Greeting Rodriguez near a small wood shack, he led him in for a formal introduction.

There was generally a protocol to meeting Chapo Guzmán—kisses, blessings, little fawning gifts—but perhaps unaware of the usual decorum, Rodriguez took a seat and launched into his pitch. Warming to his subject, he boldly proposed what amounted to a top-to-bottom upgrade of the kingpin's communications. The rooftop satellites would have to go, he said, and in their place he would bring in Wi-Fi by running cables from the biggest nearby city and extending the signal through a series of repeaters. Once this hardware was installed, he could connect the mountain compounds to the virtual private network he had built for the Cifuentes family. Opening his laptop, he demonstrated how all of it would work. Virtual private networks use normal public Internet servers, but transmit data secretly through hidden tunnels accessible only to those who have a code. With this new setup, Rodriguez explained, Guzmán would be able to send anonymous texts to anyone who was also on the network. The messages would not only be encrypted; they would be untraceable.

Even if the kingpin understood these suggestions—and it's not clear that he did—he seemed unimpressed. As an initial matter, he didn't want to merely join the Cifuentes family's system; he wanted one of his own. Moreover, he didn't like to type on his devices; paranoid and more or less illiterate, he preferred to talk. He also hadn't heard much about his cherished cordless phones, which gave him a range of more than two miles. Despite his lack of technical expertise, Guzmán had always been a shrewd consumer of technology. Over the years, he had availed himself of the best and latest from multichannel walkie-talkies to state-of-the-art scrambling equipment. He had once spent more than five million dollars on a countersurveillance scanner that he thought might help him intercept the government's own communications. On occasion, he had even paid Mexican cell-phone companies to scrub his private numbers from their files.

Rodriguez's proposal did not seem up to his exacting standards and he told the young Colombian to come back in a few more weeks to continue the discussion.

Then, as abruptly as it started, the meeting came to an end.

If he was being prudent, it was for good reason: personal security. Guzmán, distrustful to his core, tended to be wary of outsiders and strangers. That was for good reason too.

For the past eight years, a succession of generals had chased him in the mountains and while none so far had caught him, a few had gotten close. In his third year on the run—2004—the Mexican Army had managed to tap his satellite phone; two hundred paratroopers swooped down on one of his hilltop ranches, missing him by minutes. The following year, pressing their campaign, the troops arrested his eldest son, Iván Archivaldo, in Jalisco, and then one of his brothers at a family celebration at a Chinese restaurant in Culiacán. In 2006, the latest commander on his tail—General Rolando Hidalgo Eddy— upped the ante further, planning an audacious raid on the rural estate that Guzmán had built for his mother in La Tuna. Eddy had gotten word from an informant that the kingpin would be visiting the villa, a red-shingled mansion nestled in the hills that ringed the village. But when the soldiers stormed the house, Guzmán was nowhere to be found.

No matter how doggedly the military hunted him, however, Guzmán had far less to fear from his foes in uniform than from his friends in the cartel. At the time of his meeting with Rodriguez, he was embroiled in three separate wars with three separate sets of old friends. The bloodiest and most personal war was with his oldest friends, the Beltran-Leyva brothers.

The brothers—Arturo, Hector, Carlos and Alfredo—had been raised up the road from La Tuna in the nearby village of La Palma and for many years, their lives had mirrored Guzmán's. They, too, had started their careers as small-time poppy farmers and had, like Guzmán, gone to work in their young adulthood for the Guadalajara drug cartel, the reigning power of the eighties. All of the men were connected by a clannish bond of loyalty. When Guzmán was imprisoned for killing Cardinal Ocampo, the Beltran-Leyvas sent him the cash he used to procure the lobsters and liquor that lessened his ordeal behind bars. After he escaped from prison, they joined his federation of regional traffickers, serving as founding members of the Sinaloa cartel. The Beltran-Leyvas supported their old friend in his early wars of conquest against his rivals on the border, the Gulf and Tijuana cartels. The family's youngest sibling, Alfredo—virile, brown-eyed and fulsomely bearded—was especially close to Guzmán, having married one of his cousins.

The origins of cartel civil wars tend to be obscure. But Guzmán's war with the Beltran-Leyvas seems to have emerged partly out of ordinary business disputes and partly out of the kingpin's own acute anxieties over security. Throughout much of 2007, the two sides had been sparring over a lucrative distribution route in Chicago. Arturo Beltran-Leyva, the family's leader, was also still seething over the painful losses he had suffered that year when nearly twenty tons of a joint share of cocaine—worth hundreds of millions of dollars—were seized by the American authorities from one of Mayo Zambada's merchant freighters. Heightening the pressure, Guzmán had become displeased with the mounting control that Arturo and Alfredo were exercising in Acapulco, a profitable port town he wanted for himself. Then, in late 2007, another new general, Noé Sandoval, began a tour in Culiacán and like his predecessor, Eddy, stepped up operations, closing airstrips, seizing small planes and destroying pot and poppy fields.

Up in the mountains, Guzmán did not appreciate that Sandoval was harassing him while down in Culiacán the Beltran-Leyvas were living the high life, carousing freely and conspicuously turning up at lavish parties with famous singers and soap opera stars. The tensions broke into the open in January 2008 when Sandoval's troops, suddenly switching targets, went after and arrested Alfredo. Arturo, who was prone to fits of cocaine-fueled rage, immediately blamed the arrest on Guzmán. Mayo Zambada, playing a familiar peacemaking role, convened a hasty summit, denying that his partner had tipped off the authorities. But a few months later, when Guzmán's son Iván was released from prison on a curious technicality, Arturo, already suspicious, decided that the fix was in. After that the two men's friendship was, as Mayo's brother, Rey Zambada, put it, "Not as comfortable, if you will." Another one of Guzmán's intimates, his chief of staff, Damaso López Nuñez, had a slightly more pointed assessment of Arturo. "No one could make him come to reason," he said. "He decided . . . to make war."[6]

Even for Mexico, the bloodshed, which began that April, was unprecedented. Violence ripped through Culiacán: in May alone, more than a hundred people in the city lost their lives. Some were burned to death; some were beheaded; some were raked by gunfire while waiting for a traffic light to change.

Among the dead was one of Guzmán's sons. On May 8, well after dark, Edgar Guzmán López was coming out of the Forum shopping mall in Culiacán with a few of his friends when three SUVs screeched up in the parking lot, blinding them with headlights. The young men ran toward their own truck—a bulletproof Ford—but not before a dozen gunmen opened up on them. Even for a gangland hit, the killing was excessive: five hundred rifle rounds were fired and nearly twenty vehicles were damaged or destroyed. One of the killers had been armed with a bazooka.

In the wake of Edgar's murder, a stone cross flanked by flowers and a legend reading "We Will Always Love You" sprung up in the middle of the shrapnel-strewn lot. Rumors swept through Culiacán that

6. One more thing may have infuriated Arturo: namely, that Guzmán, by arranging for Alfredo's arrest and Iván's release, had beaten him at his own game of conspiring with the authorities. While the Beltran-Leyvas were accomplished traffickers in their own right, the family's specialty had always been the acquisition of intelligence through bribery. By the time of their war with Guzmán, the brothers were already paying off at least one top drug official and had a mole inside the army who provided them with President Felipe Calderón's daily schedule. They were also said to be assembling a syndicate to raise as much as fifty million dollars to bribe Genaro García Luna, a former federal police officer serving as Calderón's public security director. It was typical of the siblings that when Alfredo became enraged after one top general refused his offer of a three-million-dollar bribe, Arturo told him not worry: he himself was paying off a general of higher rank. Alfredo wanted to kill the general who turned him down, but in the end his brother convinced him to chop up a few stray dogs and leave the remains outside the general's barracks.

Guzmán himself had come down from the mountains and was holed up in a stupor at a house he kept in town. For the funeral, it was said, he bought every rose in the city and blocked the streets around the mortuary where the young man's body lay so that he could grieve in private. Despite his savage narcissism, Guzmán was profoundly connected to his family. Even in the frantic days after he escaped from prison, he had managed—at great personal risk—to visit his mother in La Tuna. But Edgar's death was particularly painful. He was only twenty-two, a business student and the father of a newborn baby girl.

It was only a matter of time before Guzmán took revenge. Still in mourning, he returned to the Sierras and sent out waves of kidnap teams with orders to find and "lift" high-value Beltran-Leyva targets. One of the suspects was discovered within days. Alex Cifuentes was in the mountains when the man was flown up to one of Guzmán's camps to face interrogation. The kingpin, solemn in a baseball cap, was waiting at the airstrip as the plane came down, sitting judge-like at a small white table in a clearing. The man was hauled in front of him, already bloodied by a beating. As the questions started, Alex looked away for a moment; when he turned back, the man's severed head was lying on the ground.[7]

Christian Rodriguez returned to the mountains in the new year. When he arrived in the Sierras—flying in from Medellín then up from

---

7. The other conflicts, occurring simultaneously, pitted Guzmán against the Tijuana cartel and the Juárez cartel. The battle in Tijuana reached back to his fight with the city's leaders, the Arellano-Félix brothers, beginning in the early 1990s. The war in Juárez had begun more recently. In 2008, Guzmán sent an invading army into Juárez hoping to seize the city from its longtime chieftains, the Carrillo-Fuentes family. Like all of Guzmán's military efforts, these wars were motivated by a combination of personal animus and business interests. Both the Arellano-Félix brothers and the Carrillo-Fuentes brothers were former friends and native Sinaloans who had run afoul of him. More important, the cities they controlled were lucrative border crossings with easy access to the vast American marketplace.

Culiacán in another small plane—he saw that Guzmán had taken his advice: the Internet cables and repeaters were in place and the camp had high-speed Wi-Fi. The young technician had done his own work in the interim. Over the past few weeks, he had scrapped the idea of putting Guzmán on the Cifuentes family's network and had instead devised a plan to connect a group of high-tech cell phones to a separate server network. Working in tandem, the phones and servers would give the kingpin exactly what he had asked for: the ability to talk in secret through the Internet, not just to send encrypted texts.

Rodriguez's new system was a triumph of complexity. The cell phones he planned to use—Nokia E-71s—would transmit voice data back and forth through Guzmán's high-speed Wi-Fi. The data would be guarded as it moved from phone to phone by three locked "doors" that could be opened only with a keycode. One of the doors would protect the encrypted conversations as they left the phones, another as they reached the network's firewall and a third as they passed through the central server headed toward their final destinations. Most of the Nokias would—for ease of use—have three-digit speed-dial numbers, like desk extensions at a company. Mindful of the kingpin's complaints about his cordless phones, Rodriguez had sketched out plans for a digital adapter permitting those devices to work on the system too. There would also be a second server—a trunk, he called it—attached to the central server; it would enable calls from the networked phones to those that were not directly connected to the network.

If the basic structure was intricate, only an advanced engineer would understand its detailed working parts: SIP vendors, private branch exchanges, TLS encryption. Which is why Rodriguez brought along a visual aid this time. Sitting in the shack again, he spread his flowchart on the table, mapping out the system for Guzmán, Alex and the head of their technical department, a heavyset man nicknamed El Gordo. Here, he pointed, was the server he was planning to build for the Nokia extensions. And here, as they could see, was the adapter for the cordless phones. Over here was the trunk he wanted to add, which would connect the Nokias to the rest of the world.

Once again, he performed a demonstration, booting up his laptop and connecting his own phone to a prototype server in his office in Colombia. When the line was open, he placed a call to Dolly Cifuentes and passed the phone to Guzmán.

It was just a silly test—"Hi, can you hear me?"—but the kingpin seemed to like it. There he was, in the middle of the mountains, talking to his friend *through a computer.*

Approving the project this time, Guzmán offered Rodriguez one hundred thousand dollars on the spot to do the job. Half he would get now in cash, half would be sent to him in Medellín.

With fifty thousand dollars in his luggage, Christian Rodriguez hurried home and got to work. In a matter of weeks he had roughed out the network, and all that remained was to configure the extensions. When Alex Cifuentes called with a list of people Guzmán wanted to have access to the system, Rodriguez began assigning speed-dial numbers. The kingpin got 121. His eldest son, Iván, got 129. Mayo Zambada was given 150.

There were other people too and Rodriguez was familiar with many of them by now: Guzmán's chief of staff, Damaso López (125); his lawyer, Oscar Gomez (145); and his favorite ex-wife, Griselda López (132). Soon, however, the kingpin started calling to add more people to the list, some of whom were not familiar. There was Muchacha (126), ING (122) and someone named Raton (135). Within about a month, the list had grown to nearly seventy names.

Rodriguez needed help and was relieved when Alex's assistant offered to lend a hand—it was an oddity of Guzmán's operation that the kingpin's private secretary had a small staff of his own. The assistant, Andrea Velez, had been on Alex's payroll for a year, but didn't seem like the rough-edged flunkies Rodriguez had encountered in the mountains. A Colombian like he was, Andrea was stylish, cultured and well educated; she had gone to a prestigious Catholic girls' school in Colombia, then on to university where she had obtained a psychology degree. As they worked together setting up the Nokias in a swimsuit shop that one of her girlfriends owned in Medellín, Andrea shared her story. Not all of it, of course—no one in the kingpin's inner circle spoke too openly. But just enough for Rodriguez to get a sense of how she had found her way into the same precarious universe that he had.

Andrea had first met Alex a year ago, she said, after moving to Cancún. Before that, she had been living in Miami, but unable to find a job in the economic downturn after the American recession, she had taken a chance on Mexico, which had seemed like an adventure at the time. Andrea had a friend in Cancún, a Colombian actress named Angie Sanclemente, and when Angie introduced her to her boyfriend, Alex, Andrea recognized him as one of the Cifuenteses, a wealthy family of Colombian entrepreneurs. Alex loved pretty women and quickly hit it off with his girlfriend's friend, offering her a job as his assistant. The job seemed glamorous and easy enough and Andrea had accepted.

It was all fairly normal for the first few months. Alex owned four or five apartments in the heart of Mexico City and one of Andrea's earliest assignments was to spend his money filling them with art and Hermès furniture. When he decided to improve his look, Andrea took him shopping. Alex spent a good deal of time in the Mexican Sierras, and whenever he was up in the mountains, he often asked Andrea to send him little odds and ends—mostly outdoor gear from Bass Pro, his favorite camping shop. It was, she knew, somewhat curious that all of these transactions were in cash and that every now and again Alex had her drop by luxury hotels to pick up packages on his behalf. But at least in the beginning, it was only part-time and she didn't really think about it much. Andrea had a day job, a good job, doing advance work for the well-known political consultant J. J. Rendón. On the side, she pursued her other passion: running a modeling agency.

It was only when she was brought into the movie project that she finally understood what was going on. The project had been Angie's idea: as an actress, she knew scripts and had always wanted to make a film about Alex's famous boss. Several months earlier, she and Alex had pitched the boss on the idea and convinced him to hire a writer, someone from Colombia who Angie knew through the industry. The writer, Javier Rey, had started on a book—*El Padrino*, he was calling it—since that was how it worked. You had to have a property in hand before anyone would think about your screenplay.

As Alex started to trust Andrea, he put her in charge of corresponding with Rey. Soon enough, she discovered who the book was about—and who she had been working for in secret all along.

But that, of course, was the one part of the story that Christian Rodriguez already knew.[8]

He had made his own discovery by that point: life in Guzmán's entourage was anything but normal.

A few months after the encrypted cell-phone system was in place, the kingpin summoned Rodriguez to another meeting in the mountains. Even by his own clandestine standards, the subject was exceptionally sensitive.

When the young Colombian arrived, Guzmán sat him down again

---

8. Andrea's account of how she came to work for Guzmán may be slightly self-serving. It is certainly the case that Alex Cifuentes, like the rest of his family, held himself out as a legitimate businessman, and it was not common knowledge at the time that he and his siblings were working with the kingpin. But the hints were there to be seen, if Andrea wanted to see them: the endless cash lying about, the hotel pickups, Alex's trips to the Sierras, where Guzmán was known to be living. It would hardly be unusual if, with good money coming in, she chose to ignore these things.

with Alex and his tech chief El Gordo and asked him what he knew about spyware. Rodriguez knew enough to recommend a product called FlexiSPY, a commercial software designed to be uploaded onto cell phones and computers. As the three men watched, he opened the kingpin's laptop and logged on to FlexiSPY's website. Once you installed the program onto someone's phone, he said, the malware gave you access to everything they did: you could read their texts, see the records of the calls they made, obtain their GPS locations. FlexiSPY organized this data into handy spreadsheets that were automatically emailed once a day to the registrant's account. There was even a feature that made it possible—legally and with a click—to activate a cell phone's microphone remotely. That meant the kingpin, if he was interested, could eavesdrop in real time on the conversations of the people he was bugging.

Guzmán was interested. The sensitive part was who he wanted to bug: his wife, his ex-wives and several of his girlfriends. He had always been preoccupied with what people said about him publicly and even more with what they thought about him privately. From the earliest days of his career, he had wiretapped his lovers, friends and enemies, and had long maintained a cabinet stocked with secret gadgets: little pens and calculators equipped with hidden transmitters. Even Alex, as devoted as he was, thought that he was paranoid, always probing everyone around him for signs of disloyalty and betrayal.

FlexiSPY was exactly what he wanted and he told Rodriguez to get to work at once.

They were ready within a matter of weeks: eight or nine BlackBerries infected with the FlexiSPY malware. Once the program was installed on the phones, Rodriguez completed the paperwork, setting up the usernames and registering the licenses. When the first of the accounts went live, Guzmán disappeared for a while, poring over pages of his lovers' texts and phone logs.

It was bad enough at first that Alex and El Gordo started to joke that FlexiSPY had become his new toy. But to Rodriguez, the program must have seemed more like an obsession. Every day, sometimes more than once a day, the kingpin called to complain that the GPS on one of the bugged devices wasn't working or that another had gone silent altogether. The spreadsheets of data, meanwhile, were becoming so voluminous that Guzmán turned them over to one of El Gordo's subordinates on the tech team. The young man, Benjamin, was ordered to read through the reports each day and write up detailed summaries on anything suspicious. To be sure that no one knew what he was doing, Guzmán instructed him to sit at his computer wearing headphones and pretend that he was listening to music.

It only got worse. In the early months of 2009, Guzmán approached Rodriguez again to ask if it was possible to intercept emails from an Internet café. As they discussed the project further, it turned out what he really wanted was to intercept every email from every Internet café in Culiacán. This was a preposterous request: There were hundreds of thousands of people in the city and who knew how many Internet cafés. It was also a mission without an explanation: Guzmán rarely gave a reason for the duties he assigned.

Rodriguez reached his breaking point that spring. One day, he was sitting in his quarters when a red alert rang out that the army was approaching. There were procedures for events like this and at the sound of the alarm, the kingpin's security detail hurried into action. The gunmen in his personal guard grabbed their heavy weapons and the two external rings established a perimeter and started to surveil the troops from posts along the roads. Amid the panic, Alex found Rodriguez and quickly hauled him toward the edge of camp. Guzmán, dressed in camouflage, was already there receiving updates. As the field reports came in, he issued an order for everyone to move a little farther up the hillside. They would run if they had to; but until they had determined where the soldiers might be headed, it was safer, he advised, to remain in place and hope they simply passed.[9]

They all fled when the army came into the compound, slipping off in file down a narrow mountain path. That first afternoon, they walked until nightfall, sleeping in a small house in the woods, twenty of them bedded down together. On the second day they walked again, stopping only to take shelter in a canyon out of sight of the helicopters hovering above them. When one of the gunmen caught Rodriguez staring at his weapon—a very large weapon—he bravely boasted it could shoot the helicopters straight out of the sky. But if he meant to be comforting, it had the opposite effect. Rodriguez was in pieces, worn down by the walking and rattled by the kingpin's crew of killers who were armed to the teeth with he didn't even know what. It didn't help that Guzmán seemed oblivious to danger, hiking through the wildflower scrub in a trance of self-assurance. Alex kept the young man close. But by the third day, when they reached another house and were put on trucks for the long ride to back Culiacán, he was near the point of collapse.

Rodriguez never returned to the mountains. Flying back to Colombia, he stayed in touch with El Gordo and his tech team at a distance, answering their questions by phone or email. As he settled back into life in Medellín, he found it difficult to keep the ordeal of the past year to himself. Not that there was anyone to talk to. While he might have confided in Andrea Velez, she was still tied to Guzmán's organization. Unable to contain himself, he turned to a friend, or

---

9. Isaias Valdez Rios, aka Memin, served as one of Guzmán's guards for several years starting in 2004 and described the kingpin's security protocol thusly: "All throughout the mountains, the different towns, everyone had CB radios. And they were actually telling you constantly, 'Hey, the *guachos*, the military people, are on their way.' There were people who would actually let us know they're on their way, they're coming closer. . . . So we would just simply step aside so that they would go by."

rather an associate, a fellow resident of Medellín he had worked with in the past.

The associate was one of those men who always seemed to attract new opportunities; and after he had listened to Rodriguez tell his story, he generously shared one with his friend. Something, he said, had come to his attention: a freelance project in New York, just the sort of thing that might prove easy—and lucrative—for someone of a technical bent. A Russian organization was looking for a communications system, something like the network that he had built for Guzmán. The Russians didn't want a long-term relationship; they wanted a product, at a reasonable price, no strings attached. If Rodriguez was interested, the associate could make the introduction. All he had to do was fly to New York and meet one of their men. After showing him the system, he could turn around and fly right back to Colombia. With, of course, a big bag of cash.

THREE

Keys to the Kingdom

February 2010–February 2012

When Christian Rodriguez flew to New York in February 2010, the Russian seemed as promised: He was a man with simple needs and a suitcase full of money. If he looked a little menacing with his scowl and leather jacket, it was how those people were. The two men's business was conducted quickly, their conversation technical in nature. Rodriguez had brought along an off-the-shelf encryption system, not quite a generic model, but nothing fancy either: a standard product that any businessman might use if he was traveling and wanted to speak securely with the office. To the casual listener, their meeting would have sounded much like what it was: one man selling technology to another in a hotel room high above Times Square. Rodriguez showed the Russian how the system worked—*press alt-A, now hit 7*—and how to configure the cell phones he was buying. A few delicate issues were discussed, but only to establish bona fides. The Russian said that he and his partners mainly worked domestically, moving merchandise from one state to another, a fine operation, but much more modest than the technician's other customers'—if he had his facts straight. Cautiously but audibly, Rodriguez admitted that the Russian's facts were straight enough. He had indeed done work for the drug lord Chapo Guzmán.

Sitting in the suite next door, Marston and Potash had him. The camera and bug mic hidden in the Russian's room had caught it all on tape. Throughout the meeting, the agents had been tuned in live through the audio feed and monitor, fascinated to have heard Rodriguez confirm his connection to the kingpin and to have gotten their first real glimpse of a man who until then had only been a shadow. The two men arrived at similar conclusions: that Operation Server Jack might actually work. And that Christian Rodriguez, while certainly a genius, wasn't much to look at.

Then, as they sat watching, the target they had tracked for months took his money and walked out the door.

It had always been the plan to let him go. While Marston and Potash now had the means to charge Rodriguez with aiding and abetting— maybe even with conspiracy—the higher-ups at C-23 were of the opinion that a hard sell wasn't possible. If they had stormed the room, threatening indictments, it would have likely spooked the young man and kept them from their ultimate goal of getting him to turn on Chapo Guzmán. A formal arrest would have also required going public with his name, which would have placed Rodriguez in extraordinary danger and risked alerting the kingpin that they were on to him as well. It wasn't easy watching Rodriguez leave, but Marston and Potash knew that they were closing in on their prize—the keys to the kingdom, as they had started calling it. Better to hang back, the squad's more reasonable minds advised, and lie in wait for a sounder opportunity.

Hanging back might have been easier if there had been some progress on the technical end. But whenever the agents made another call to

ERF, they got the same answer: *Almost, but not yet.* Marston and Potash didn't know how many times they had driven down to Quantico
by now. While they couldn't blame the techs, it was maddening to
hear that they didn't know much more about the Nokia at this point
than they did on the first day they had had it.

Hacking into the server had also hit a wall. The IP address was still
a moving target, flitting from place to place with no discernible pattern. Even worse, every time that ERF thought it had a way into the
system, the components seemed to change. First, the phones on the
network had been upgraded—from E-71s to E-72s. Then the server
itself had changed, or rather other servers had been added to the system. There was one on the network that now appeared to have been
designed for BlackBerries. No one knew what *that* meant.

The Associate was able to shed a little light on it. In speaking with
Rodriguez, he had heard a whisper about some sort of spying or surveillance project. It wasn't quite clear what this project was, but it
seemed to be a kind of internal security effort that Guzmán put in
place to monitor his people. Other than that, most of what the Associate was offering were random little tips about where Rodriguez was
going, what he had been doing and how he was feeling about his job
with Guzmán. Though he hadn't been to the mountains in months,
he was still employed by the kingpin, on safe ground in Colombia.

With Rodriguez at home and ERF's tech team at a standstill, Marston and Potash reassessed. They were still collecting everything they
could about Rodriguez and took what they could get—or whatever
judges gave them with a warrant—rooting around in the young technician's emails and sifting through his purchases on Amazon. But
even though they knew Rodriguez had developed Guzmán's network,
they were not persuaded that he was the best or the only source who
could help them crack it. After scratching at the edges of the young
man's circles, the agents had stumbled on to two more possibilities:
the kingpin's other techies, El Gordo and his partner, Charly Martinez.

Marston and Potash started digging into their lives too with the same assiduous attention they had lavished on Rodriguez, all the while hoping that the techs at Quantico would finally come through.

At least there weren't any naysayers now. After their coup with the Russian, their colleagues, who had formerly been skeptical, started showing interest. Had they approached the kid yet? Did they think that they could flip him? Could he really get them into Guzmán's system? The secret network, once dismissed as myth, was developing a buzz. Within the bureau—and beyond—Operation Server Jack had suddenly grown legs.

But with the legs came debates and disagreements. There were, as always in the government, certain elements with differing opinions about how they ought to handle the case. Some of them were not inclined to take the gradual approach and sit back waiting for the proper moment in which to educate the young Mr. Rodriguez about the benefits of FBI cooperation. One month after C-23 had lured Rodriguez to Manhattan, a hit team in Juárez had gunned down a pregnant American consulate worker and her husband in what seemed to be the latest atrocity in Guzmán's war of conquest on the border. If the secret cell-phone system was indeed what Marston and Potash said it was—the kingpin's communications lifeblood, indispensable to his trafficking operation—then why hinge everything on a twenty-year-old kid? Why not take a more forward course of action and shut the system down with a colossal denial-of-service attack, blasting Guzmán and his Nokias back to the Stone Age?

With the keys to the kingdom in the balance, Marston and Potash cautiously pushed back. It was not as if the kingpin's network had a kill switch they could flip. And even if there was a switch somewhere, they didn't know exactly where, or how it worked, or who could help them find it, except perhaps for . . . Christian Rodriguez. Moreover, and in a separate vein, what was likely to happen, they argued, if Guzmán woke one morning and found a 404 error flickering on the screen of his phone? Experience, and their own investigation, suggested he would just go out and hire a new brilliant techie to build him a new brilliant system and then they would be back at square one.

The whole thing was starting to take a toll. Potash found himself consumed by mysterious anxieties. Something, he felt, anything, could happen now to screw up their investigation. The Colombians might learn about Rodriguez and arrest him. Or Guzmán himself might get arrested, even killed. Neutralizing the kingpin was the point of the operation, but Potash couldn't bear the thought of someone else making the collar or never getting to hear the conversations passing through the Nokias. In the mornings, as soon as he got out of bed, he rushed to his computer and nervously checked Google wondering if months of work had already gone down the drain. It was only after he had entered his search terms—*El Chapo, captured, dead*—and nothing popped up that he relaxed.

These were hardly idle worries. Throughout the spring and summer of 2010, as the Juárez corridor exploded into an orgy of car bombs, kidnappings and mass assassinations, the authorities from Mexico to Argentina rounded up several cartel leaders close to Guzmán. Among the first to go was Luis "Don Lucho" Caicedo, who was captured in Buenos Aires in April. Don Lucho, it was alleged, had shipped nearly nine hundred tons of Colombian cocaine to American consumers, much of it through Guzmán's private smuggling routes. A few months later, the Mexican Army killed the kingpin's number-three man, Ignacio "Nacho" Coronel, in a shootout in Jalisco. In September, the Beltran-Leyva brothers' blond-haired, American-born security chief, Edgar "La Barbie" Valdez, was picked up at a house in

Mexico City—less than a year after tipping off the Mexican Marines to the location of his former boss, Arturo Beltran-Leyva. Even as Marston and Potash strategized about how and when to button-hole Rodriguez, their colleagues in the bureau's Boston office were deep into their own secret sting against the kingpin. Posing as Sicilian gangsters, agents in New England had set in motion Operation Dark Water, a covert plot to capture Guzmán moving crates of Peruvian cocaine to a port in southern Spain in a cover load of pineapples. Not only had they sent an informant to the mountains to get the effort started, they were *this* close to convincing Guzmán to come down from his hideout and personally quality-check the deal at an airfield near Madrid—at which point they were going to grab him.

In the end, what pushed the New York agents into action was another competing case: the one being run in part by their old friends from the DEA in Bogotá. In November 2010, Bogotá's work on the Cifuentes family found its way into a federal indictment in Miami. For the first time, it was revealed in public that the US government was investigating Jorge, Dolly and Alex. The charging document, which reached back to Pacho's early days in 2003, was exceedingly comprehensive: there were seizure dates; aliases for each of the defendants; and dozens of meticulously detailed financial transactions routed through American banks amounting to millions of dollars. It all suggested that DEA Bogotá and their partners in Miami had, some time ago, inserted an endoscope deep into the bowels of the family's organization.

The American indictment, based on a wiretap, was an existential threat, and the Cifuentes siblings and many of those around them started getting nervous. Just before the charges were announced, Jorge fled to Venezuela, grew a beard and hid out in a small town near Caracas, moving in with a family of local farmers. Even the more reasonable minds at C-23 decided it was finally time to hit the gas on Operation Server Jack.

They had no choice but to get Rodriguez now—before he, and a hundred other Colombians, went underground.[10]

They turned again to the Associate.

Over the course of several months, the agents' secret source had already done much for them. In his far-flung meetings with Marston and Potash, he had taken orders to coax Rodriguez into sitting with the Russian; kept his handlers apprised of their subject's movements; and provided them with the initial proof of concept phone. Now the Associate was going to deliver the technician to the FBI's front door.

Shortly after February 14, the Associate prevailed on Rodriguez to fly to Bogotá. The purpose of the trip was to have him met there, by surprise, by the men who had been trailing him since 2009. Potash had picked the date himself. It would not have been wise, he reasoned, with the ungodly hours he had been working, to be out of the country on Valentine's Day and risk further pissing off his wife.[11]

Bogotá's El Dorado Airport has a busy pickup zone for taxis just beyond the sliding glass doors outside arrivals. That was where Marston and Potash, joined by one of their colleagues from the embassy, waited for Rodriguez at shortly after eight in the morning on February 21, 2011. When the young man stepped outside, two local uniformed policemen approached him flashing badges. They told Rodriguez to come with them, please, and placed him into a car parked at the curb.

---

10. Jorge had been tipped off to the indictment by a Colombian naval intelligence officer who paid him a visit shortly before the Miami case was unsealed. In a shocking breach of security, the officer, who has never been named, not only had a copy of the still-secret indictment, he also had some of the wiretap recordings.

11. The FBI has never said what pretense the Associate used to convince Rodriguez to fly into Bogotá. Perhaps it doesn't matter. What matters is that even before the young man boarded the plane, Marston and Potash had the details of his flight.

It was one of the smallest cars that the Americans standing nearby had ever seen.

Potash went first, climbing in through the back door on the passenger side. No doubt shocked to see a *gringo* in the car, Rodriguez started sliding toward the driver's side and was met by the agent from the embassy sliding in beside him. In the crowded back seat, Potash pulled his own badge out and introduced himself as an American federal agent. He told Rodriguez they needed to talk and asked for his permission to take him somewhere quiet. When Rodriguez, looking ashen, nervously assented, Potash asked his hosts if they could find a place nearby for a private conversation.

They ended up at a seedy motel a few blocks from the airport. No one had to show ID and they paid the clerk in cash. Rodriguez took a seat inside on an armchair across from the couch and coffee table. The room was small, not much bigger than the car outside, and the agents squeezed around their subject. All of them avoided going anywhere near the bed.

The pitch by the Americans was candid and direct. They knew who Rodriguez was, they said, what he had been doing and exactly who he'd done it for. They also knew that he wasn't really a criminal; he had just fallen in with the wrong crowd. Marston and Potash played to the young man's image of himself: He ran a business, needed money, it was perfectly understandable. But the sort of people he was dealing with, they quietly assured him, were not the sort of people that he wanted to be dealing with, not if he was interested in living into his thirties. To be clear he understood that they were serious, they showed a few cards: Charly Martinez? The man he had trained to run the network in his absence? Yes, they were aware of him. Rodriguez seemed most comfortable when Potash talked to him about the servers and encryption keys. That made sense. Then it wasn't simply about the kilos and the killings; it was about technology.

When they brought things to a point—the business of cooperation—

Rodriguez was in a kind of trance, staring at the embassy agent's sidearm tucked into the holster at his shoulder. The agent was leaning forward like the rest of them, hands on knees, waiting for an answer, his service pistol swaying back and forth like a hypnotist's pendant. Someone was telling Rodriguez it was time to come on board, time to make a decision, he should help them, help himself. Snapping out of it, Rodriguez said all right, he would do it. To celebrate, they all climbed back into the little police clown car and drove off to the Marriott. Taking a suite, they ordered room service and waited for a bigger team from the embassy to arrive.

There was, however, one more matter to discuss. In the motel near the airport, Rodriguez had admitted to almost everything. He had talked about the work that he had done for the Cifuentes family. He had described the system he had built, down to its smallest details. He had even, grudgingly, acknowledged building a similar system for someone else, a bigger and more powerful criminal boss. The one thing that he had not yet done was utter Guzmán's name.

Marston and Potash had never seen fear like this before. They kept going back to the question, gently then firmly explaining that they knew he'd worked for Guzmán. All Rodriguez had to do, they said, was just admit it. By now, it was after dark and they had all been at it for nearly eleven hours. But it was almost as if Rodriguez was choking: he couldn't breathe and was gagging on the name.

Eventually he spat it out, like something from his lungs. And as soon as the syllables hit the air—*El Chapo*—the pressure seemed to lift. Rodriguez looked like he had just expelled a toxin from his body. His breath came back, his shoulders loosened and he sank into his chair. While Potash sat with him, Marston got up and went to call their bosses in New York. Getting them on the line, he said he couldn't make a promise yet, but it seemed like the Colombian was in.

An hour later, they let Rodriguez go for what was now the second time. He had to catch his flight back to Medellín, he said; his family was expecting him. Before the young man left, Potash gave him a private cell phone preinstalled with a local Bogotá number. He told Rodriguez that he and Marston would be there for a while and Rodriguez agreed to come back in a day or two to meet them.

Then he was gone—forever, Potash feared. After a restless night, Potash woke and sent the text.

Good morning. How are you?

For a long while, too long, there was nothing. Then—*bloop*—there was an answer.

I'm good. How are you?

Potash was also good, exceptionally good. It appeared that the Colombian was definitely in.

In the final days of February 2011, FBI confidential source Christian Rodriguez flew by way of Miami from Medellín, Colombia, to New York City for a series of debriefings at the bureau's field division office at 26 Federal Plaza in Manhattan. The interviews, conducted by the source's handling agent, Robert Potash of Squad C-23, touched on matters ranging from his professional experience as a hacker and technician to his historical relations with several members of the Cifuentes family, known drug dealers in Colombia. The sessions also included an account of Rodriguez's more recent involvement with Joaquín "El Chapo" Guzmán, a leader of the Sinaloa drug cartel believed to be hiding in the Sierra Madre mountains in or near his birthplace village of La Tuna. Rodriguez stated that he had met Guzmán on numerous occasions in the mountains, primarily through the auspices of Hildebrando "Alex" Cifuentes, the Cifuentes family's

youngest member. He also attested to building Guzmán three dis-
crete Internet servers as part of an encrypted cell-phone system that
was used in the furtherance of trafficking activities.

Potash did his best to keep Rodriguez calm during the hours
they sat talking in the room in Lower Manhattan. But it was clear to
him that the young man was a wreck. How could he not have been,
caught between the FBI and an international drug lord? In Colombia,
Rodriguez said at one point, you couldn't trust the cops—they weren't
any better than the traffickers. He eventually confessed that in the
small motel near the airport, when he had been staring at the other
agent's pistol, he had actually been terrified that they were going to
kill him.

Potash was distressed. But at least for the moment, he wanted to
move things on to the question of next steps. And it seemed that the
next steps were going to be difficult. Rodriguez had already thrown
a wrench in the machine: while the young technician had acknowledged that he had built the kingpin's secret servers, he also said that
he no longer had access to the data they contained. As a technical per-
fectionist, he had designed his hardware in the most secure fashion,
allowing Guzmán and his men to set their own passwords without
establishing an overriding master code. Even if Rodriguez wanted to,
he couldn't just crack into the secret phones at will. Potash had imagined that with Chapo Guzmán's personal IT guy at his side, it was
going to be easy. All they would have to do was flip a switch and the
intercepts would start rolling in. But clearly, he realized, that wasn't
going to happen.

It now appeared that they would have to start from scratch
and build a whole new system. Rising to the challenge, Rodriguez
had a few ideas of how to make it work. For security purposes,
he said, his three current servers bounced around constantly
through different data centers and whenever he needed to move
them, he would tweak the components. If they were going to build

new servers, he could simply tell Guzmán that he was making another move and that this time one of the tweaks required resetting passwords. Then, when they placed the system in its new location, he could insert a script into the network. The script, he explained, would peel the passwords off and quietly send copies to both him and the FBI.

Yet again, Potash was impressed. And with a plan in place, he and Marston saw Rodriguez off: the young man was eager to go back to Medellín and get to work. The agents, in the meantime, went about their own work, deciding on a place to house the system once Rodriguez finished it. They both assumed that Guzmán would be wary if they moved his servers, which were now located in Canada, to the United States. But if the servers needed to be moved—in order to tweak the system without arousing suspicion—there were several reasons to put them in the Netherlands. The country's combination of strict privacy laws and lax drug statutes would, they theorized, probably appeal to the kingpin. It also didn't hurt that the FBI had a close relationship with the Dutch police's special cyber unit, the High Tech Crime Team. The HTCT, which had offices and a cutting-edge wire room in Driebergen, just outside of Utrecht, had long been one of the continent's top online investigative squads.

As prosecutors in New York drafted a request to the Dutch, the agents' own squad ginned up a web of fake identities to serve as cover in the public-facing aspects of setting up Rodriguez's new system. When the phony names and credit cards were ready, Marston and Potash used them to rent space at a Leaseweb server farm in Haarlem, a massive complex of generators and satellite antennae large enough that their covert operation would likely go unnoticed. Working with the Justice Department, they sent their letter off to Holland, asking permission for HTCT to tap into the system's three IP addresses: one for the Nokia server (95.211.10.70), another for the trunk server (83.149.125.226) and a third for Guzmán's BlackBerries

(83.149.125.227). The letter, which effectively performed its legal function, was slender on investigative details. It referred, obscurely, to the confidential source at the heart of the operation as Individual-1 and only revealed that he lived in Medellín and had built an encrypted cell-phone network for the drug lord Chapo Guzmán.

It could easily have taken Rodriguez months to build the network, but working manically at home in Colombia, he completed it in not much more than a week. When Potash saw the final product, he wasn't just impressed this time—he was profoundly impressed. The young man had developed what amounted to a mesh of soft servers hidden in the shell of a hard machine. Only the inner core—a series of Linux virtual devices—was visible to unsuspecting users; no one who didn't know that it was there would even think to look for the external Windows casing. That was the genius of it all: Guzmán's other techies, El Gordo and Charly Martinez, could log into the system the same as always and wouldn't have a clue that the outer digital crust was monitoring everything they did. As long as they didn't check the server logs too closely and catch Rodriguez sneaking through a back door to tinker with the innards, they wouldn't—and couldn't—figure it out.

With the system finished, all that remained was to wait for a moment when Rodriguez could suggest the idea of moving it to the Netherlands. Given how the kingpin's business worked, it didn't take much time. In early March 2011, one of Guzmán's low-level operatives—a man known as El Pariente—was arrested. El Pariente had a phone extension on the current system and Potash recognized the opening. He told Rodriguez to approach the kingpin gently and propose a range of security measures in the wake of the arrest. First, he should suggest wiping El Pariente's phone clean. Then he should advise updating the system and moving it from its present location. Finally, as an extra precaution, he could recommend resetting all the passwords.

It was the young technician's first exposure to working under-cover, and though it was fairly simple, no one knew how he would handle it. But helped along by an infallible assistant—Guzmán's own distrustful nature—he managed in the end to stumble through just fine.

The switch in the Driebergen wire room was flipped on the morning of April 6, 2011. Within a matter of days, the emails with the intercepts started coming in.

C-23 had been waiting months for this but when Marston and Potash pressed play on the audio files, it all came out as unfathomable chatter. Their translators went to work at once, but no one knew what to listen for at first. Rodriguez helped them pick out Guzmán's voice. But even then, whatever he was saying—and he was saying quite a bit—was dense and cryptic, full of references to unknown people and unknowable situations. They were finally in the kingdom, and had found it was a crazy maze of unfamiliar rooms and people speaking an impenetrable language. Listening to the intercepts was like pass-ing by a window on the street and catching little snippets from the middle of a conversation between strangers.

April 14, 2011, 7:46 p.m.

JGL: That bastard Meño is abusive. Isn't there a way to get him? Where is he?

M-10: They have him over there. . . . I believe Felipe has him in Phoenix.

JGL: He hurts them from over there? That bastard . . . from all the way over there?

M-10: No, well. . . . He had a big office. . . . He got them out, and put them in the office with the ones with Flaco Salgueiro.

Every so often things made sense. In those halting early weeks, as the Dutch sent more and more emails to New York, Marston and Potash picked up crumbs about ranches in Canada, tunnels in Mexicali and what seemed to be an airstrip in Costa Rica. Guzmán, it appeared, was drowning in these details, dealing with an endless string of managerial issues. One of his operatives had recently asked if he could reroute some product from Los Angeles to his customers in Ohio. Another had complained about a new police commander in Durango. The commander wasn't following his orders and the local team had already been in contact with the governor. Perhaps the boss would consider making a call.

The agents were surprised. They had expected someone different: coarser, tougher, a Mexican Scarface with a booming voice and an abrasive personality. But the man whose calls they were now receiving once or twice a day had a high-pitched, almost whiny, accent. He also seemed to be reasonable at times.

April 9, 2011, 2:18 a.m.

JGL: So then . . . you beat up those policemen?
CHOLO: I kicked their asses, the federals, all of them. . . .
JGL: And what did they tell you?
CHOLO: What are they going to say? . . . They were fucked.
JGL: Don't be so harsh . . . Cholo. Take it easy with the police.

Marston and Potash were surprised by something else: there wasn't much on their wire about drugs or drug dealing. The intercepts were filled with office gossip, shocking talk about corruption and salacious prattle about sex, but there weren't many of the usual indicators of a trafficking operation: pickups, drop-offs or kilos crossing the border. They felt a bit deflated: as drug cops, they were primed to find drugs, and they wondered if they might have missed something or if Guzmán had managed to slip one by them. But after hashing it out with their colleagues, it dawned on them that the kingpin wasn't using his encrypted system to run the bulk of his daily operations. The phones were being used for something different: to run the corporate structure of his business.

Not that the epiphany helped much with the bosses, some of whom were demanding quick results. There was, in the FBI, a standard way for handling a wiretap: You obtained a warrant, you listened for a while and then you went into the grand jury and nailed your targets with the evidence. As the resident techie of the squad, Potash found himself having to explain that the system they had set up with Rodriguez was not a standard wiretap. First, he noted, it was exceedingly complex: there were cell phones here, BlackBerries there; Windows was intermixed with Linux; servers were stacked on other servers; and all of them sent and received their data in slightly different ways. Imagine it like this, he heard himself saying more than once: We've designed our own phone system, run by our own phone company; we've put it in a foreign country under totally different laws and then we've let the bad guys think that they're in charge, when in reality we've been sneaking in each night, stealing all their calls.

When he put it that way, people usually got it. But even so, the explanation barely scratched the surface of the perils and complexities of keeping the whole thing going. Rodriguez's network, while certainly ingenious, could be glitchy. Marston and Potash had noticed from the start that when they opened some of the emails from the Dutch, the data was garbled and unusable. At other times, they could hear the calls, but only one side of the discussion was recorded. (*Yeah . . . On Thursday . . . No, his cousin's house . . .*) The other half was often somewhere else, in a completely different email. To match the separate parts and weave them back together required the techs at ERF to write complicated algorithms.

They finally figured out that the system wasn't acting up; it was their partners in the Netherlands. In July 2011, HTCT confessed that they hadn't been collecting Guzmán's calls as they were stored inside the servers; instead, they'd been collecting the calls after they had left the servers. By that point, the network's software had already diced the conversations into encrypted bits of data. It was no one's fault; the Dutch police were simply following their laws, which prosecutors had interpreted to mean that only calls in real time—and from one phone to another—could be captured. To accommodate these laws, Rodriguez came up with a workaround. With his access as the network's administrator, he slipped into the system one night and inserted another script. This script routed everything through a blind, third-party conference call. The conference function was invisible to Guzmán and his men. But since it permitted the Dutch to technically take part in the calls, it complied with the restriction of only monitoring live conversations.

But even this solution, as savvy as it was, was not entirely flawless. A few weeks later, Marston and Potash went back to the Dutch with a new request. This time, they wanted HTCT to break into the first two servers—the trunk and cell-phone servers—and make full imaged copies of their preencrypted contents. That way, they assumed, they would get everything on the network. It took a while for the Dutch to figure out if that sort of hacking was legal in the Netherlands; and even once they determined that it was, they realized that since the first two servers were inextricably connected to the third BlackBerry server, they needed an additional request to copy that one too. The process started taking so long that Marston and Potash asked for something else: permission for Rodriguez to build another server, one that would copy all the others and store their data as backup. Finally, they thought, all of Guzmán's calls would now be legally, and technically, accessible.

All of this, of course, was on top of the risk they ran in getting caught by Guzmán's in-house tech team. Maintaining the system was a round-the-clock ordeal. The servers were like heart pumps; if they ever stopped running—or so the New York squad room liked to say—the patient would immediately die. Whenever Rodriguez went into the network to fiddle around with something or implant a line of code, he tried to do so late at night or early in the morning when Charly Martinez and El Gordo were likely to be sleeping. If, as he often was, he was making his fixes from New York, he tried to hide his footsteps on a map of anonymous pathways. Rodriguez had inserted a program into a system that would automatically clean the administration logs each night so that no one knew he had been tinkering. But the program wasn't foolproof. One day, he woke up and saw that the auto-erase function had failed. There his log-in was—from a US address—for anyone to see.

When he reached out to Potash in a panic, it was Marston who talked him off the cliff. Call El Gordo, Marston said. Call him right now. If he suspects that something's wrong, the last thing he'll do is take your call.

Rodriguez called El Gordo. And, thankfully, El Gordo took the call.

After months of this—the late-night patches, the vexing legal hold-ups, the working out of various little kinks—the intercepts suddenly slowed down. By late August 2011, Guzmán's personal calls had already dipped dramatically. Then, in December, the rest of the system more or less ground to a total halt. The Dutch, by that point, had sent Marston and Potash nearly two thousand calls. Minus hang-ups, about eight hundred were actual conversations. Of those eight hundred, Guzmán himself had been captured on about two hundred. No investigator, in more than twenty years, had ever caught the kingpin talking live on two hundred individual phone calls. Now, however, just as it seemed like they were finally getting going, he was gone.

Sitting in New York, Marston and Potash were befuddled. They didn't understand what was going on. The Guzmán they had come to know was a capricious customer, especially when it came to high technology. It often seemed that he was easily bored and was always on the lookout for the latest innovation. Late in the winter of 2011, there were two of those in the communications world: iPhones and BlackBerries. The iPhone had sex appeal: it was shiny, sleek and so-phisticated. The BlackBerry, which the kingpin already had, offered something different: simplicity and security. Most people didn't like to talk on BlackBerries; instead they typed their messages by hand. Maybe, the agents mused, Guzmán was going through a natural evo-lution and had moved from the Nokias to different toys and tools. Maybe he didn't want to drive his '87 Honda anymore and wanted something new.

Whatever it might be, if he wanted something new, they were going to give it to him. With help from Rodriguez, the agents put together an-other set of servers designed to work with iPhones. The iPhone servers had all the bells and whistles that the Nokia servers had—encrypted voice on an encrypted virtual network—with the addition of some new ones: encrypted text and Internet. Launching a kind of guerrilla marketing campaign, they had Rodriguez go to Mexico and demon-strate a mockup of the iPhone for Guzmán's techies, Charly Martinez and El Gordo. But no matter how ardently the young man promoted the iPhone, Guzmán wasn't interested. In a little twist to Operation Server Jack, Alex Cifuentes was.[12]

---

12. That, at least, is the FBI's story. There was, however, another twist to the story: the involvement of the Central Intelligence Agency. While the full account of the CIA's role in Guzmán's case is buried in secret files, the agency appears to have been work-ing closely with Marston and Potash about the time they fed Rodriguez's iPhones to Alex Cifuentes. The nature of the partnership remains unclear. It is possible that the wiretap that was ultimately placed on Alex's phone was assisted by the CIA. It is also possible that one of Langley's assets helped persuade Alex to take the phone in the first place. The FBI's intelligence cousins may indeed have been assisting Marston and Potash as far back as their initial discovery of Christian Rodriguez and the Associ-ate. Only three things can be said for certain: The bureau has declined to discuss the

A natural-born hanger-on, Alex had spent much of his life admiring and imitating more formidable men. The chance to have his own private cell-phone network—one that resembled Guzmán's, but was newer and improved—was too much to resist. He took Rodriguez's product almost from the moment it was offered. And as soon as he had the iPhone in his hand, he started texting like a lovesick teenage girl.

Scrambling to capture this cyclone of messages, Marston and Potash rushed yet another letter to the Dutch, asking H7C7 to start recording Alex's iPhone servers too. By January 2012, the intercepts on Alex were already pouring in and it became obvious that despite his glaring flaws, Alex was a major player in Guzmán's global empire. He appeared to be in charge of much of the kingpin's Canadian operations and was deeply enmeshed in his businesses in Ecuador, where his own brother Jorge had worked for several years. It did seem somewhat curious that even though Alex was more or less a glorified assistant, he had his own assistant, Andrea Velez, who, the tap suggested, traveled for him to Canada and Ecuador and was buying all his furniture and bedsheets. Then again, Alex was curious himself. As Marston and Potash soon discovered, he had recently moved to the resort town of Cabo San Lucas, where, it appeared, he kept a witch doctor on personal retainer. Alex was obsessed with everything occult: UFOs, the Illuminati, pyramids on Mars. Paging through his texts about giant aliens or the planet Nibiru may not have been enjoyable. But if it kept them close to Target Guzmán, Marston and Potash would do it.

*   *   *

CIA's involvement in the case; the agency responded to a Freedom of Information Act request by saying that its role—or lack of a role—was a "currently and properly classified" matter; and several US officials, including one from within the FBI, said that the relationship existed.

That had been the goal all along: to stay close to the kingpin, get him back. Marston and Potash had already failed to lure him with the iPhones. Now they tried the BlackBerries.

It was actually Rodriguez's idea. Just before the Dutch had started to spy on Alex, the young technician approached his handlers, mentioning a sensitive, long-term project that Guzmán had him working on. Some time ago, he told them, he had been asked to insert malware FlexiSPY onto several BlackBerries the kingpin handed out to his wives and girlfriends. More recently, Rodriguez said, Guzmán had come back to him with new instructions to install the spyware onto thirty more devices—not only for the women in his life. The kingpin had just discovered that one of his top lieutenants, his cousin Juancho Guzmán, was an American informant, and that may have triggered his natural paranoia. Now he wanted to avail himself of FlexiSPY to bug his lawyers, his security chiefs and several of his closest aides.[13]

Marston and Potash immediately recognized the possibilities. The FlexiSPY data Guzmán was collecting was invaluable. If they could get their hands on the private texts and physical locations of dozens of people in his innermost circle, it would be like looking at a photograph in negative of the kingpin's life itself. They jumped into the project straight away.

But within a few days, they encountered several roadblocks. FlexiSPY, as they found out, was based in the Seychelles, an island chain in the Indian Ocean that lay beyond the reach of American subpoenas. Moreover, its proprietary data was housed on cloud servers owned by Amazon in Washington State that were managed by a separate firm in Texas known as Cloudflare. Both of the companies

13. Juancho Guzmán's body was found by Mexican authorities on December 15, 2011, mouth taped, facedown, lying on a dirt road on the outskirts of Culiacán. Several cartel figures later testified that Chapo Guzmán had him killed.

told the agents to get lost when they called for help in tracking the data down. Theoretically, the Justice Department could have girded up for a six-month legal battle, and might have even won it. But Marston and Potash were in no mood to wait for litigation. They told Rodriguez to use his access to the program to quietly download Guzmán's FlexiSPY files onto the FBI's own Amazon server. Then, with the trove of data in their hands, they asked their prosecutor, Christian Everdell, to submit an application to a judge in New York, begging for permission to inspect it.

In late December 2011, the judge came through and Marston and Potash got the go-ahead to pry into Guzmán's FlexiSPY accounts. Opening the downloaded files, they were stunned by the raw amount of data. The GPS coordinates alone that Guzmán had gathered on the targets of his spying went on and on for pages. FlexiSPY had been tracking their locations for the kingpin—down to the decimal degree—on an almost hourly basis for a month, and there were dozens of targets in dozens of accounts. Twenty-four hours a day, multiplied by thirty days a month, multiplied by as many as forty targets—it was tens of thousands of numbers. Guessing there was gold in there, Potash spent that weekend making macros in Excel. When he overlaid the data onto a map, he saw that there were hot spots for Guzmán's underlings in two of the usual places: Culiacán, his urban base, and his other favorite hideout, the rugged mountains north and east of the city. There was a third hot spot, however, in an unexpected place: Cabo San Lucas, where Alex Cifuentes had been living.

As overwhelming as the locational data was, it was nothing compared to the written messages they found inside the download. In terms of sheer page numbers, the FlexiSPY texts were even more voluminous—screen after screen of never-ending BlackBerry chats. Through his constant spying, Guzmán had amassed an encyclopedia of his crews' communications, and yet they were remarkably obscure.

Perhaps the kingpin knew what they meant, but Marston and Potash didn't.

> **3:26 P.M.:** My friend here wants to know if you can start talking to the man—that if we buy him a boat—if he would be willing to fish in Los Angeles, and willing to receive 200 miles out from San Diego. And as to the material . . . which one, of the small ones or the grass?
>
> **3:31 P.M.:** Of the small ones.

It was fairly clear that the people who were sending these messages were talking about drug deals. Unlike the Nokia intercepts, the FlexiSPY chats were filled with constant references to money, merchandise, phone numbers, bank accounts, airplanes, airstrips, factories and front companies. But it was far from clear who the senders were or what, exactly, they were doing. All of them were using little code names—Mona, Riris, Poy—which made it impossible to identify anyone conclusively. Even more confusing, they weren't sending their texts back and forth on ordinary phone numbers; they were using BlackBerry Messenger, or BBM, the company's internal chatting system. BBM swapped chats in a wholly different way: based on hard-to-track alphanumeric PINs.

A photograph was indeed emerging from the data, but it was out of focus. Unlike the voice calls the Dutch had intercepted, the FlexiSPY texts were effectively anonymous.

And endless.

After Rodriguez got them the first batch of malware downloads in December, there were two more batches in January. Potash tried his best to keep it all straight on his Excel sheets: one for the GPS coordinates, another for the texts. But by early February, he had already amassed nearly two hundred thousand digital locations for members of Guzmán's crew and enough of their BlackBerry chats to fill a novel. The whole thing—all of it—was madness: a daft game of double-layered espionage. Marston and Potash were spying on the kingpin even as he spied on large swaths of his own organization. Guzmán's jealousy and paranoia had buried the FBI in data.

That same month Marston and Potash caught a break that helped them cut through this morass, and it came from an unlikely place: the DEA. Just as the flood from FlexiSPY was rising past their necks, they got a call from the agency's elite investigative unit in Chantilly, Virginia: the Special Operations Division, or SOD.

The guy from SOD had something for them: a BlackBerry PIN. A few days earlier, he said, a DEA task-force officer in San Diego had, as part of a long-term investigation, stopped one of Chapo Guzmán's girlfriends at the border as she was passing through the San Ysidro crossing. The officer, Juan Sandoval, had squeezed the girlfriend for information and, fearing arrest, she had given him the PIN, claiming it was Guzmán's personal number. Sandoval was a solid cop, the SOD guy said, with deep lines into the kingpin's sons, wives and mistresses. He had immediately sent the number to the embassy in Mexico, but you know how that often went: the embassy got all kinds of crazy shit on Guzmán. The BlackBerry PIN had made its way back to SOD and when the unit ran the number through the deconfliction system, which tracked ongoing cases across the federal government, a hit popped up for Marston and Potash in New York. The SOD guy was guessing that the PIN might be part of their own long-term investigation, the one the agents had briefed Chantilly on not long ago.[14]

---

14. SOD's recollection of the conversation, while similar, differs in a few key aspects. The unit had in fact been briefed on Operation Server Jack, though only, its agents say, after a certain amount of pushback from the New York FBI. "We were super impressed by their level of infiltration and by their informant," said one of the division leaders at

Hanging up, Potash went directly to his computer. Opening his Excel sheet of FlexiSPY texts, he hit Alt-F and typed in the digits of the PIN he'd just been given. The search function churned and spat back its results as a yellow rash of highlighted splotches. The Black-Berry PIN—Guzmán's PIN—was everywhere in the data.

Potash hollered for his translator and he hurried over to read the highlighted messages. It *was* intriguing, the translator said. There was no way to be certain, of course, but given the context of who this PIN was talking to and the nuance of the slang it used, it could be, if they didn't hold him to anything definitive—

Is it him or not? Potash interrupted.

Oh yeah, the translator said, it's totally him.

It just made sense. The PIN that SOD had sent along often used the not-so-subtle screen name "J" and appeared to be in charge of most of the conversations it took part in. Many of these conversations were business conversations: chats about sending pilots on passport-less "black flights" or incorporating companies in Germany to buy pre-cursor chemicals from China. But some of the chats were personal in nature and even more revealing. For the next few days, Marston and Potash plugged in Guzmán's name wherever the PIN appeared, and a whole new world emerged. They read about the kingpin's home reno-vations and the plastic surgeries he had purchased for his mistresses. There were glimpses of his lawyers, his pilots, his father-in-law, even of his young wife, Emma Coronel, giving voice to their twin infant daughters, Kiki and Emali.

---

the time. "But we left with an understanding that they were going to share their intel with us on Chapo's subordinates so that we could do our own exploitation." When information from Marston and Potash's wiretaps was given to SOD, however, it was "garbage," the former leader said: mostly insignificant tips on irrelevant low-level tar-gets. SOD arrived at the conclusion that Marston and Potash, while paying lip service to the notion of sharing intelligence, were actually attempting to maintain the secrecy and integrity of their wires.

2:07 P.M.: I want my little princesses here to fix my meals.

2:08 P.M.: Yes, daddy. What do you want us to make you? Enchiladas? Or maybe it's best if mommy makes them for you, after all, it was her enchiladas that made you fall in love with her.

Surfacing from all of this, Marston and Potash were dazzled. They had jumped into the FlexiSPY data thinking they would come out with a negative of the kingpin. Instead, they had stumbled onto what amounted to a high-resolution color portrait. It simply hadn't occurred to them that the program's malware would have picked up Guzmán's own texts along with those of all of his many targets. But there they were, exposed for all to see and still stored in the system.

The two of them could not believe their luck—or his stupidity. In his fits of suspicion, Guzmán had managed the impossible.

By wiretapping everyone around him, he had accidentally wiretapped himself.

FOUR

Red Hombre

In search of sun that winter, the kingpin Chapo Guzmán went on a holiday in Cabo San Lucas, flying in to the fabled beach resort on a private plane that landed in the cactus-studded hills above the coastal strip of luxury hotels. Joining him was one of his most trusted aides: his bodyguard and secretary, Carlos Hoo Ramírez. A former helicopter pilot with a brush cut and a slim English mustache, Hoo Ramírez—better known as Condor—had been at Guzmán's side for years, watching his back, handling his phone calls and generally clearing paths around him. Lodging for the two men had been arranged by an advance team in a split-level, salmon-colored mansion with a large perimeter garden and a red-tiled roof at the end of a cul-de-sac in Punta Ballena, one of Cabo's most exclusive gated communities. The vacationers were traveling light, with only a cook, a pilot and a gardener in their entourage. Guzmán had demanded that a treadmill be installed in the house for daily exercise. But other than that, there was not much to distract him: a deck with lounge chairs, a teardrop swimming pool and glittering ocean views.

After ten years of living in the mountains, the kingpin had grown weary of his secluded highland camps. Whenever his safety and schedule permitted it, he loved slipping off to havens like Los Cabos where he could eat well, drink among his friends and have his pick of the local professional talent. Now was a good time to have gotten away. In recent weeks, the bloodshed and beheadings of his expansionary war in Juárez had started to devolve into a frustrating stalemate. At the same time, a new conflict with a new foe—his former allies, the Jalisco New Generation cartel—was slowly heating up in Guadalajara. Not more than a month or two ago, Guzmán had gotten word that twenty-six of his men had been slaughtered in Guadalajara, their bodies heaped into three vans parked near the Millennium Arches. Nearly simultaneously, another sixteen soldiers had been discovered burned to death—some of them in handcuffs—in Culiacán. On Christmas Day, the army had arrested one of his top security chiefs, Felipe Cabrera. Then there was the nastiness involving his cousin Juancho.

In Cabo he could forget about all that—or try to. When Guzmán arrived in the city, he shed his mountain camouflage and made his way through the palm-treed streets in blue jeans, Nikes and a baseball hat. Behind the tinted windows of his gold Suburban, however, the sports pack he carried was still filled cautiously with hand grenades. Condor accompanied him everywhere he went with the launcher tucked in his guitar case.

Three days after the revelation that they had Chapo Guzmán's Black-Berry PIN, Marston, Potash and Christian Rodriguez boarded a flight to Mexico City. The spur-of-the-moment trip had been prompted by a phone call that the FBI agents made to their counterpart at SOD in the wake of their discovery. It was a courtesy call, or so they thought, to let the team at the DEA know that they were right: according to the bureau's intercepts, the BlackBerry was in fact connected to the kingpin. The call in turn had set off a windstorm that had blown from Chantilly, through Washington, DC, all the way down to Mexico and back in less than seventy hours. Though Marston and Potash didn't know the details, they soon found out the bottom line: the DEA, leveraging the BlackBerry PIN, had drawn a bead on Guzmán and was planning a raid.

A meeting had been set up, pending their arrival, at the embassy. First, however, Marston and Potash booked Rodriguez into a hotel: they didn't want to march their confidential source through the front door of one of the most public buildings in the city. Since leaving Manhattan, Rodriguez had been furiously working on his laptop, monitoring Guzmán's FlexiSPY accounts for any breaking intelligence. Once they settled into their rooms, he gave his handlers the good news—and the bad. The good news was that it seemed as if the kingpin hadn't gotten wise to their surveillance and was still using the PIN in their possession to send chats back and forth. The bad news was it was impossible to know with any certainty if the physical device connected to the PIN was actually in his hands. Rodriguez had seen the process firsthand: Guzmán rarely touched the BlackBerries he used, preferring to have his bodyguards do his texting for him. They—and the BlackBerries—might, or might not, be standing next to him at any given time.

When Marston and Potash arrived at the meeting, they found the usual embassy Who's Who: the ambassador's staff, the DEA's regional director and his men, and some people from the bureau's legal attaché team. As the New York agents took a seat, they presented themselves as wanting to be useful. They admitted that they didn't work in Mexico and didn't know the landscape or the players. They also said that they would not presume to insert themselves into the tactical details of a ground operation that required coordination with the Mexican authorities and was, as a drug raid based on foreign soil, the province of their DEA colleagues. They did, however, suggest that they had something valuable to bring to the table: the FlexiSPY data and the expert technician who had managed to collect it.

The DEA felt differently. By its lights, Marston and Potash had not come down from New York to offer their assistance in capturing the kingpin; they had instead come down to talk the embassy out of the mission. The agents based in Mexico might indeed have heard the two New Yorkers acknowledge that they weren't versed in Mexican affairs—an opinion they agreed with—but they also heard Potash say that it would be ludicrous to launch a raid on Guzmán now when C-23 was still receiving intelligence on the kingpin and, moreover, had an undercover source in a risky situation in the field. In the DEA's assessment, Marston and Potash had staked out an inflexible position: they seemed to believe that keeping the FlexiSPY data coming in was more important than going after Guzmán since it could ultimately lead to taking down his entire organization. Then again, the DEA's own position was equally unwavering: Possessing information but failing to use it, they insisted, was an exercise in futility. And they already had their own information: the BlackBerry PIN that Juan Sandoval had gotten from the kingpin's girlfriend.

This second version of the meeting was not quite the cooperative summit that the first one had seemed to be. And it ended with a few strong words from the DEA.

You can do your own thing, if you want. Because we're sure as hell going to do ours.

January passed in a blur of beachfront business.

Though supposedly on vacation, Guzmán spent his afternoons and many of his evenings at the house in Punta Ballena hunched above his

BlackBerry. Like any chief executive, he was inundated by messages from the office. Among the swirl of projects that required his attention was a new meth lab he was setting up in Ecuador and a large load of cocaine that was already in transit from an airstrip in Belize. Toward the middle of month, he checked in with his father-in-law, Inés Coronel, about a different load they were moving through Nogales, Arizona. Guzmán advised him to situate his couriers correctly and to please stay off the radio since the Border Patrol was listening. A few weeks after that, he was dealing with an issue in Detroit where his local cell needed more storage for their inventory, and handling the fallout from a hitch in San Diego. One of his truck drivers there had somehow lost the keys to a trailer full of merchandise, setting back delivery. In Phoenix, meanwhile, longtime clients had reached out with an urgent order for weed. Even as he struggled to fulfill the request, he learned that one of his panga boats had been seized off the coast of Santa Barbara. When he subsequently found out that three of his boatmen had also been arrested, he started making arrangements to find them lawyers.

All of this, and more, was on top of the domestic matters he was dealing with at home. Earlier that winter, he and his wife, Emma, had started making plans to build a house in Culiacán, a trophy mansion with a master suite, three guest bedrooms and quarters for the maid. Every few days, he was on his BlackBerry reminding her to be sure she told their architect to put high ceilings in their own room and to design the shower with an extra-wide stall. In between discussing these instructions, they often found time to talk about their two infant daughters—no, he would not be back to celebrate their birthday—and to share the various details of their private lives. Emma was having trouble deciding on a present for a good friend who had given her her own lavish gift—a twelve-thousand-dollar Rolex. When she asked her husband for a budget, he told her that she shouldn't spend any more than eight thousand dollars. While Emma was grateful, she was on a diet preparing for plastic surgery, and it sometimes made her testy.

12:24 P.M.: I can't eat and I'm starving. . . . Are you going to chat with me . . . or will you be busy?

They mostly lived apart these days, and whenever Emma flew in from Culiacán to visit him in Cabo, she rarely stayed at the house in Punta Ballena. Instead she stayed with Alex Cifuentes, at his own house, a ten-thousand-square-foot villa across the peninsula in Pueblo Bonito. There, she and her daughters could spread out and enjoy themselves while not intruding on her husband's other business. Alex was busy too, of course, overseeing the kingpin's routes in Canada and the manuscript project with the writer Javier Rey, who had spent much of the spring and summer working at the property. But unlike his employer, Alex knew how to relax. An amateur astronomer, Alex spent hours each day taking pictures of the sky and many of his nights gazing at the heavens through the high-tech telescope Andrea Velez had bought him for his birthday. Alex's house was fun and full of visitors—not just Rey and Emma, but the lovely gay couple that Andrea had hired to design the website for Alex's pet side project, a wind-powered real-estate development up the coast in Baja. On winter evenings when Guzmán was too caught up to join them, some of the guests would sit for dinner on Alex's rambling deck overlooking Sunset Beach. The meals were spectacular, served by the infinity pool and cooked to perfection by their host's private chef.

Finding Guzmán, as the DEA well knew, had always been the easy part. Communications were so essential to his operation that there was always surveilled intelligence that could pinpoint his location.

The hard part was different, and twofold: First you had to figure out, once he had been found, if it was even possible to grab him. Then, because of the corruption in the government, you had to determine who in local law enforcement could actually be trusted with the grabbing.

As February 2012 hurried toward an end, both questions fell to Victor Vazquez. Vazquez, a veteran agent based at the embassy in Mexico, had been on duty the day Juan Sandoval had called in with his tip about the BlackBerry PIN. Though many of his colleagues had been skeptical, Vazquez tended to believe it. He knew Juan Sandoval, had worked with him in San Diego and trusted him implicitly. A former Marine, Vazquez approached his job at the DEA with a ramrod rigor and a sense of personal mission: he was after all a native Mexican, born in Durango, a state that bordered Sinaloa. After talking things over with Sandoval, Vazquez went to work checking out the BlackBerry PIN with sources of his own. Within a few days, he had run the information to the ground.

It wasn't simple turning PINs into locational coordinates, but Vazquez had a man in Guadalajara who, for a price, would quietly run the numbers through the Mexican telephone system. The results came back as a map: on the map, a little red *hombre* marked the place where the PIN had left a ping. When Vazquez got the map for Guzmán's PIN, he was shocked to find the red *hombre* standing in what seemed to be a condo complex, a few miles inland from the coast in Cabo San Lucas. Cabo wasn't Culiacán, the kingpin's stronghold city, and it certainly wasn't the mountains. Cabo was a party town with nightclubs, bars and million-dollar villas.

Christ, thought Vazquez, we could do this. Staring at the red man on his map he could not believe his luck.

The guy was on vacation, taking sun and chasing girls, like every other idiot at the beach.

*   *   *

Or perhaps not *chasing* them: Guzmán's girls usually went to him. One of them arrived in Punta Ballena in February, around the time that Emma and his daughters left for home.

Slender, dark-haired and twenty years his junior, Agustina Acosta was a lawyer by profession, but in her year or so of dating Guzmán she had started to perform a different role. The kingpin was always searching for new ways to insulate himself and had a habit of running much of his business through his mistresses. Not long after Agustina met him, she became both his lover and his personal assistant.

In many of the projects Guzmán was involved in, Agustina handled all the details. Serving as his go-between, she would toggle back and forth on the three separate BlackBerries he gave her, fielding questions from his customers and underlings and responding with his answers when she got them. Already that winter, Agustina had helped her lover set up his meth lab in Ecuador, negotiate the purchase of the chemicals he needed and supervise the movements of a ton-sized shipment of cocaine to Arizona. When Guzmán's panga boat was seized in California, Agustina did the grunt work and looked into the public defender who was representing his boatmen. Ruthless and resourceful, she seemed to have a special knack for cracking the whip on his workers when they shirked or dragged their feet. The screen name she used in her private chats with Guzmán was "Fiera"— the Wild Beast.

Her compensation for all of this often came in the form of personal courtesies: the liposuction treatment, for example, that Agustina underwent, and that Guzmán paid for, just before she flew to meet him in Cabo. Though she was still recovering from her surgery—her waist hurt to the touch—she landed at Los Cabos International on February 16 and quickly made her way to the house in Punta Ballena. Driving in from the airport, she bantered with the kingpin, coyly priming him for their reunion. *I'm on my way, love. I'll be with you in ten.*

Agustina was smart—certainly smarter than most of Guzmán's girlfriends. She understood his need to be flattered and had no problem lying to him or coddling his ego. Aware of his paranoid nature, she had also assumed from the start that he was spying on her.

A week before she checked into the hospital, she confided to a friend that something seemed to be wrong with the three phones he had given her—never suspecting how right she was or how wrong they really were.

5:14 P.M.: I don't trust these BlackBerries. . . . The bastard can locate them.

Having located the bastard, Vazquez and his colleagues now turned to the second part of their equation: finding someone to go after him in Cabo.

Under Mexican law, American agents were not allowed to act alone in ground operations in the country. This traditional restriction required them to work in tandem and to share intelligence with law enforcement partners whose loyalties were often undiscernible at best. From the embassy's perspective, police work in Mexico was frequently a guessing game where you had to choose the least untrustworthy counterpart and hope that when you turned around, they didn't simply stab you in the back. It could feel at times like performing surgery through a kind of proxy doctor—one who might have been quietly paid off to kill both you and the patient on the side.

After much discussion, Vazquez and his DEA partners settled on a strike force, cobbling one together from the local Cabo SWAT team and a special squad of federal officers who were based in Mexico City. There had been some conversations early in the process about bringing in the Mexican Marines, elite troops from the navy with a reputation for probity and ruthlessness. But on top of corruption, there were questions about rivalries to consider. And the Marines didn't always get along with the police.

Vazquez had to admit, it was not ideal, having two separate elements under the command of two separate officers—neither one American—chasing the little red *hombre* through Los Cabos. Then again, it was not ideal that the FBI had shut their Colombian source in a hotel and refused to bring him anywhere near the embassy.

But that was how it always was in Mexico: the tools in the toolbox were simply what they were.

In his hotel near the embassy, Christian Rodriguez waited fifteen minutes then pressed refresh again.

He knew that FlexiSPY was able to transmit updates from the king-pin's BlackBerry faster than that—at short five-minute intervals—but he also knew that increments that frequent would probably wreak havoc with its battery.

With the capture mission imminent, the young man had been tasked with keeping watch on Guzmán's messages and his GPS coordinates through the program. The last thing he wanted was to overplay his hand and cause the kingpin's BlackBerry—the only way to track him—to suddenly go dead.

Refresh—still there.

Refresh—still there.

Refresh, wait. Refresh, wait.

Refresh.

At shortly after nightfall, on the evening of February 21, two hun-dred officers from the Cabo SWAT team and the federal police moved out from their staging grounds at the international airport. Tracking Guzmán's BlackBerry PIN, they drove in a convoy toward a gated community of fifteen or twenty new adobe homes clustered in a neighborhood near the center of the city, a few miles from the water.

As the two police teams made their approach, they were unexpectedly joined by the Mexican Marines, who had belatedly decided that they too wanted to take part in the mission. What had at first been a hybrid operation with two different forces and commanders now had three.

When the triple-pronged assault team closed in on its target, armed men from each started going house to house, breaking down doors and hauling people more or less at random on to the street.

Back at the embassy, Victor Vazquez and Juan Sandoval waited for a follow-up report from the ground commanders on their group chat. The initial report had been somewhat less than promising. The strike teams, it had been confirmed, had not found Guzmán yet, although the search continued—was continuing. As for the residents who had been taken from their homes, it seemed that they were mostly elderly expats from the United States and Canada. Many, in their broken Spanish, had made it clear they weren't pleased.

Vazquez and Sandoval didn't get it. They could see the red *hombre* standing on their map: he was right there, where the police were, where he was supposed to be. The sneaky bastard Guzmán must be hiding. Try the closets, they told the commanders, then try the basements and the kitchen cabinets. Search under the goddamn rugs—he had to be there somewhere.

Except he wasn't there. Not at shortly after nightfall. And not hours later at four in the morning.

By the time the mission ended, at a little before dawn, the only thing the teams had discovered were a few more angry *gringos*.

* * *

In the morning, over breakfast, Marston and Potash ran through the possibilities. The raid had been a failure—that much was clear. But now what?

They had to assume that Guzmán had gone back into hiding or was already on the run and that at any minute, the FlexiSPY devices they'd been tracking might, like the Nokias, also go dark. A single botched op, they began to fear, was about to obliterate three years of their work.

But then the phone rang. It was Rodriguez. The young technician was in his room, looking at the spyware spreadsheets. Though he didn't understand it and couldn't quite explain it, everything seemed normal.

Normal how? Marston and Potash wanted to know.

Regular normal, Rodriguez said, normal normal. The flow of messages, the GPS locations—none of it had changed.

The agents' disappointment flipped into bewilderment. What they should have been seeing—had expected to see—was a flurry of activity on FlexiSPY: panicked texts about troops busting in on the condo complex; orders issued to dump communications; some kind of movement, however slight, in the kingpin's coordinates. But there was none of that—not even a hint.

It didn't make sense, but the data was the data. And the kid was right: the data looked . . . *normal.*

The little red *hombre* hadn't moved. It didn't make sense.

On the morning after the raid, Vazquez went back to his man in Guadalajara. But even when he ran the PIN again, the ping was still there, in the exact same place. *Mira*, he said, referring Vazquez to the map. *El hombre rojo, mira.* Yeah, Vazquez almost told him, fuck your *hombre rojo*—there wasn't anything there.

The embassy was scratching its collective head. Some agents theorized the PIN was bad; others that their man in Guadalajara was taking them for a ride. Whatever it was, Vazquez figured that Chapo Guzmán was the luckiest *pendejo* in Mexico. But the thing was this: he had to be lucky all the time; they only had to be lucky once.

After his colleagues had run out of theories, Vazquez called the one man who could help him sort it out. Brian Maxwell, of the United States Marshals Service, was the leader of a classified tracking team that had been working in Mexico for nearly a decade. Maxwell—everyone called him B-Max—was an expert in both finding fugitives and bringing them in, and had taken part in countless snatch-and-grab operations against major cartel chieftains. B-Max's specialty was signals—surveillance and countersurveillance—which meant he got to see not only the government's most secret tools for hunting miscreants, but some of the tools that the miscreants used to get away.

When Vazquez told him about the little red man, Maxwell had his own theory. Their source in Guadalajara had probably pinged Guzmán's BlackBerry number off a cell tower. But cell-tower pings were notoriously hard to read and weren't always accurate. They often gave a general perimeter, not a precise location. Maxwell had his own means of homing in on such locations and was happy to give it a try.[15]

Even with the help, Vazquez didn't want to leave a stone unturned. After signing off with B-Max he went upstairs in the embassy to see his cousins in Central Intelligence. He said he had a BlackBerry he was looking for. Perhaps, he asked, they might consider putting a plane in the air and helping him track it down?

By late that night or early next morning, the pair of stones that Vazquez overturned revealed the same worm: a new target. This

15. Maxwell declined to discuss what technology he used for this. But it was almost certainly a cell site simulator like DRT Box or StingRay. The devices send out signals that mimic those given off by cell towers and essentially suck up locational data from cell phones being targeted.

one looked to be a twenty-minute drive from the last one and lay at the edge of the perimeter in which the little red man had been standing. It was another, smaller condo complex, a cul-de-sac of sorts, with three houses clumped together at the end of a road looking out across the water.

Punta Ballena, it was called.

A few hours after the target was discovered, Marston, Potash and Rodriguez left Mexico City. The operation over and their work complete, they packed their bags, hopped a plane and flew back to New York.

It was only when they landed and the embassy reached out to them that they received the news: the mission to capture Guzmán had continued—was continuing.

Back in Culiacán, Emma was worried about him. She had heard bad news and sent a text.

2:40 P.M.: Honey, some guys in La Guadalupe Victoria were killed just now. Was it any of your people?
2:41 P.M.: No, darling.

That was a relief.

2:44 P.M.: I love you, love. Talk to you soon.

She should have been more worried.

Less than an hour later—at 3:35 p.m.—a smaller strike team of fifty policemen and a dozen more intelligence officers drove up the road toward Punta Ballena. Brian Maxwell was on the ground this time to make sure the job got done.

With Maxwell's homing equipment, it wasn't difficult to figure out which house of the three on the cul-de-sac was Guzmán's. According to the readings, it was that one over there: the salmon-colored split-level mansion with the red-tiled roof and the large surrounding garden.

Driving through the gate, Maxwell sped up the flagstone drive toward the garage. But when he and his team climbed out and turned around, the Mexicans were storming the wrong house.

By mistake? It was possible. Though it hardly seemed likely given that Maxwell was jumping up and down and waving them back toward the door that he had found. No, *amigos*, he was shouting. *This* one, not that one. *Aqui, amigos*, this one over here!

When the police finally broke into the house—the right house—they discovered and arrested three suspects: Angel Jorge López, who claimed to be a pilot; María Luisa Macías, who said she was the maid; and a slender, dark-haired woman named Agustina Acosta. A search of the premises revealed a cache of items that seemed to both confirm and refute their accounts. While the officers found a bedroom full of clothes—blue jeans, Nikes, underwear, a baseball hat—they also found an MP5 assault rifle, night-vision goggles and a sports pack filled with hand grenades.

What they did not find was Chapo Guzmán. Though after the delay by the police, Maxwell had a guess where he had gone.

Grabbing one of the officers, he ran out onto the mansion's back deck. Standing near a hedge of potted palms, he stared past the neighbor's yard toward the blue sweep of the sea.

It took a moment to find it, but there it was, behind the fronds, on the far side of the low stone wall that rimmed the swimming pool: a slightly crushed thornbush and what looked like footsteps on the sandy little path that led down to the beach.

Headed Home

As far as clues went it wasn't much to go on, except for one thing: most of the trails in Chapo Guzmán's life led back to his home in Sinaloa.

In 1957, when he was born in the small town of La Tuna, up in the Sierras, the Russians launched Sputnik, Elvis Presley was drafted by the army and *American Bandstand* debuted on TV. But these events would likely not have meant much in the far-flung village of his childhood. La Tuna was its own world then, an isolated cattle town without much indoor plumbing or a public sewage system. Its few hundred residents largely lived in poverty, many of them in simple dirt-floored homes far from the luxuries of modern schools or hospitals. The Guzmán family was no exception. The kingpin's father, Emilio Guzmán, fed his seven children on his income as a farmer and a rancher, and his wife, Maria, tried her best to keep them all in line with her pious Christian faith. With three older siblings already ahead of him, Guzmán grew up sleeping in a tomato box cribbed from the family's farmstead, where he later helped his father milk the cows and tend to his beans and maize. While his early years were not without their pleasures—hula hoops, marbles, hunting in the hillsides—life for the most part was filled with daily labor. Among the kingpin's first jobs was selling candy and his mother's bread to the neighbors. When his formal education ended in the third grade, Guzmán was put to work on the family's major cash crop: the poppies that they raised and sold for opium.

Long before there was a Sinaloa drug cartel, there were drugs in Sinaloa. The state's first opium trade reaches back to the nineteenth century when Chinese merchants who had settled in the area set up networks to grow and harvest poppies in the highlands outside Mazatlán and ship their gummy resins to dealers across the border. By the time of the Revolution, in 1910, native growers called gummers, or *gomeros*, had gotten into the business, squeezing the flowers for their pale narcotic paste and sending it north, often using smuggling routes that were later blazed during Prohibition. With the start of World War II, American gangsters, deprived of pipelines in Turkey and the Balkans, set their eyes on Mexico, and men like Bugsy Siegel created large-scale heroin operations on the state's Pacific coast. Since time immemorial, marijuana had also been a staple in the Golden Triangle, the tristate region that ranged from Sinaloa into Durango and Chihuahua. Starting in the 1950s, the sales and production of Sinaloan opium and pot were largely overseen by a young man named Pedro Avilés Perez, who was one of Guzmán's uncles.

Avilés, a doctor from the town of Badiraguato, south along the main state highway from La Tuna, was a pioneer of the Sinaloan drug trade, the first local trafficker to move his merchandise in planes to the United States and to systematically foster ties with powerful policemen. By the mid-1960s, Avilés had solidified his place as one of Sinaloa's most innovative distributors and as a chief supplier to the counterculture movements in the North. It is also possible that Avilés brought his nephew into the business of dealing drugs. In 1973, Guzmán left La Tuna—or, as some have argued, was thrown out of the house by his father—and at age sixteen took up with his future wife, Alejandrina Salazar, whom he had met a party in Culiacán. That same year, according to an interview he gave to Javier Rey, he carried out his first run as a smuggler, driving an old Ford pickup truck, packed with pot, across the American border.

Pedro Avilés was killed in Culiacán by the federal police in 1978, and his sudden death thrust the drug trade into one of its earliest periods of chaos. It is almost certain that the old-world boss was betrayed by a cabal of his subordinates. The plot to remove him was likely hatched by one of Avilés's top aides, Miguel Angel Félix Gallardo, who seized control of the underworld and ultimately served as Guzmán's second mentor.

Tall, handsome and gifted with a shrewd sense of politics, Félix Gallardo had started his career as a state policeman, detailed at one point as the personal bodyguard of Sinaloa's governor. In his early thirties, while working for Avilés, he became consumed by an ambition to improve and expand the local empire his employer had created. The Mexican drug trade was still at that point a disorganized collection of individual fiefdoms whose leaders often competed for police protection, supply chains and profitable smuggling routes. Félix Gallardo's vision was to unify the industry into a single organization. Through consolidation and economies of scale, he hoped to create a kind of supergroup that could boost production and streamline distribution while reducing violence and centralizing the handing out of bribes.

With Avilés out of the way, Félix Gallardo founded what came to be known as the Guadalajara drug cartel, which Guzmán joined as a low-level functionary in the late 1970s. It was in Guadalajara that the eager novice learned the logistics of the business, working side by side with Félix Gallardo's partners, Rafael Caro Quintero and "Don

Neto" Fonseca Carrillo. The new cartel in Guadalajara not only had creative leadership, and began growing pot on an industrial scale at vast plantations staffed by hundreds of pickers; it was also blessed with a deep bench of secondary players who would themselves eventually rise to power in the drug trade. During his time in Guadalajara, Guzmán formed significant relationships with men like Mayo Zambada and Don Neto's nephew, Amado Carrillo-Fuentes, that would last throughout his career.[16]

Everything changed—for both the Guadalajara cartel and for Chapo Guzmán—with the American cocaine boom of the early 1980s. Traditionally, the business of cocaine had been based in Colombia, where the powder was produced and where drug world titans like Pablo Escobar and the Orejuela brothers had held sway for a decade. Their business model was simple—and exceptionally profitable. Cocaine was manufactured in clandestine labs, often in the rainforest jungle, then sailed by speedboats across the Caribbean to landing points in Florida. Sometimes the barons in Medellín and Cali entrusted distribution of their product to their own employees in Miami or New York. Sometimes they contracted jobs to American middlemen.

All of this was suddenly disrupted by the Reagan administration. In 1982—one year after *Time* magazine declared cocaine "the all-American drug"—the White House put together the South Florida Task Force, a multidistrict team of nearly a dozen state and federal agencies, to crack down on the traffic from Colombia. Maritime blockades shut Caribbean shipping routes and radar planes patrolled the skies for boats that had managed to elude the naval dragnet. Within

---

16. Most members of Félix Gallardo's new cartel were, like Guzmán, from Sinaloa. The organization was based in Guadalajara, the capital of Jalisco, because in 1976 the Mexican military, helped by the DEA, chased many traffickers from Sinaloa in a violent slash-and-burn mission called Operation Condor.

four years, the task force had seized a hundred thousand pounds of cocaine, six million pounds of marijuana and racked up more than fifteen thousand arrests.

The Colombians needed a new business model; and standing by in Mexico, Félix Gallardo had one. His Guadalajaran smugglers had for years been moving marijuana across the US border and were highly skilled at negotiating the often porous two-thousand-mile frontier. Such skill came at a premium, however, and Félix Gallardo named his price. He wanted more than a shipping fee for transporting Colombian cocaine to American consumers; he wanted a percentage of the business.

It was under the terms of this arrangement that Guzmán, who was in his early thirties, became a full-time bandit at the border. While he was not at first the busiest smuggler in Mexico, he quickly proved himself to be among the fastest and most daring (his initial nickname was El Rapido). In those first years, he focused on a single border crossing—the one connecting Agua Prieta, Mexico, to Douglas, Arizona—moving his merchandise from one town to the other in family-style motor homes and later through his greatest innovation: cross-border tunnels, including one that his engineers disguised beneath a pool table. From 1987 to 1989, the American authorities estimate that Guzmán's operation passed as much as ten tons of cocaine each year across—or underneath—the Arizona border. The business earned him his initial fortune of tens of millions of dollars.

The now familiar structure of the Mexican drug trade—a landscape in which multiple cartels vie for power from separate home-base territories—started taking shape in 1989 with the arrest of Félix Gallardo and the demise of his cartel. The DEA had made the capo and his partners its primary targets in 1985, following the brutal torture and murder of a DEA agent based in Guadalajara, Enrique

Camarena. When the Mexican military tracked down Félix Gallardo four years later and captured him in Guadalajara, where he had been a frequent guest of police and politicians, his empire split apart. His allies and lieutenants each grabbed a piece of what remained—or, as some have noted, were given sinecures with his permission. Amado Carrillo-Fuentes and his brothers seized control of Ciudad Juárez. Another clan of brothers, the Arellano-Félix family, took over Tijuana. Guzmán and Mayo Zambada were granted rights to the homeland: Sinaloa and its long Pacific coast.

With a turf to call his own, Guzmán quickly flourished. He established his own relationships with Colombian suppliers, bought his own policemen and set up an extensive aerial operation that flew cocaine from southern sources to secret airstrips throughout the Mexican heartland. In the late 1980s, Guzmán employed as few as twenty people, many of them longtime friends or relatives like his older brother, Arturo. But by the early 1990s, his payroll expanded to about two hundred. While cocaine remained his profit center, his marijuana business was humming along at five to ten tons every year. He even started, cautiously, to investigate branching into heroin.

In retrospect, the first years of the nineties were Guzmán's golden years. He was in large part working under the radar, earning as much as twenty million dollars a month and plowing the profits into beach homes, Learjets, pleasure boats, zoo animals and trips to Thailand, Aruba and Macau. What he didn't spend on himself he often lavished on his staff in the form of imported sports cars and diamond-encrusted watches. Even so, there was so much money pouring in that his stash houses groaned with cash and one of his first employees, Miguel Angel Martínez, regularly went to a bank in Mexico City to make deposits from a suitcase stuffed with tens of millions of dollars. The early nineties, as Martínez once put it, were "the best thing in the world."

Success like that was bound to foster envy and dissent, and

the first place the discord started to emerge was in Tijuana wih the Arellano-Félix brothers. The nominal cause of the conflict was Mayo Zambada's decision to stop doing business with the brothers. Responding in kind, the Arellano-Félixes cut off access to the city, a crucial border crossing, to Zambada and his allies. When Guzmán stubbornly ignored their order, it ignited a skirmish that erupted into war.

It was Guzmán's first war—and it did not end well. In November 1992, the novice kingpin sent a band of gunmen to Christine, a popular nightclub in Puerto Vallarta, having received intelligence that the Arellano-Félixes would be there. Guzmán's assassins, pulling rifles from their coats, fired at the crowd, shooting out the disco lights. While they killed several bystanders—and a few enemy soldiers—they missed their target, the Tijuana leader, Ramón Arellano-Félix.

Six months later, Ramón and his brothers struck back—at the Guadalajara airport. In one of the most storied murders in modern Mexican history, Juan Jesús Posadas Ocampo, a Roman Catholic cardinal, was caught in the crossfire of a team of assassins hired to take out Guzmán. Though Guzmán escaped the hit unharmed, fleeing into the terminal then out a back door and into a passing taxi, he was blamed for Ocampo's death and a nationwide manhunt was launched to track him down. With a phony passport and a timely bribe, he managed to escape to Guatemala. But there was too much pressure to return him, and in June 1993, the Guatemalan government sent the kingpin back to Mexico, where he was tried, convicted and imprisoned.

Already wealthy and now world famous, Guzmán made the most of the eight years he spent in the Puente Grande prison, a high-security facility on the edge of Guadalajara. Through generous payments to the prison's deputy warden—Damaso López, who would one day serve as his chief of staff—he purchased a life of pampered luxury. Within the walls of Puente Grande, the kingpin enjoyed the finest food and liquor, a personal chef and conjugal visits from his wives and jail-house girlfriend. He continued to run—and expand—his business, relaying his orders on a contraband phone to his brother Arturo, who set up an apartment near his home in Acapulco expressly to receive the regular calls. Though Guzmán seethed about the Arellano-Félix brothers, who never paid a price for Cardinal Ocampo's murder, his most pressing problem was avoiding being sent across the border to face a more exacting form of justice. By the end of the nineties, he had been indicted in both Tucson and San Diego on a wide range of American federal charges. One day after Mexico's supreme court legalized extradition to the United States, Guzmán disappeared from Puente Grande.

His escape—on January 19, 2001—is a chapter of criminal lore that like the Brink's job or the Lufthansa heist has long been mired in conflict and conspiracy. Some say Guzmán slipped out of the prison dressed as a woman in a wig and high heels. Some say he paid a fed-eral judge to set him free. Some claim that he bribed Vicente Fox, then the president of Mexico, who simply let him walk out the front door. Others, with a more nuanced understanding of Mexican cor-ruption, say that Guzmán was in possession of so much dirt by then about the government's own involvement in the drug trade that he was released as a precautionary measure, free of charge.

The official position of the United States government may be the most improbable version of them all. According to this account, one of Guzmán's lawyers paid off dozens of guards at Puente Grande—those at the doors, those controlling the security cameras and those who manned the boom gate in the parking lot—to look the other way as a maintenance worker named El Chito wheeled the kingpin out of the facility in a laundry cart and hid him in the trunk of his car. Waiting near the prison was a second car, an armored Volkswagen Jetta, which hurried Guzmán through the night to a safe house in the city of Tepic. Some days later, as the military neared Tepic, Mayo Zambada, tipped off by President Fox's bodyguard, rescued Guzmán by sending him a helicopter. When the helicopter landed, Mayo's brother, Rey, drove the kingpin hundreds of miles through roadblocks and checkpoints to Mexico City, in the back of yet a third car. As the two men entered the capital, Guzmán became alarmed when a police squad car and motorcycle pulled up next to their vehicle. Rey Zambada told him not to worry. These police, he calmly said, were *their* police.

The getaway certified Guzmán as Mexico's most legendary outlaw. More important, it brought about a pivotal moment in the history of the Sinaloa drug cartel. After a celebratory party, Guzmán and Zambada, finally reunited, stayed up talking until dawn. Guzmán confessed that after his stint in prison he was broke. Zambada, like a wise older brother, told him to take care of himself and generously offered to help him out with money. The two old colleagues spoke about their business and the future of their business; and by the time the sun rose on the ranch to which they had retreated after leaving Mexico City, they came to an agreement to merge their operations into what would soon become one of the most profitable partnerships in the annals of organized crime. Vowing themselves to one another, they swore that moving forward they would split their earnings equally. "I'm with you one hundred percent," Zambada is said to have declared. "Any kilo of coke that I receive . . . I'm going to give half to you."

Once the deal was struck and sealed, Guzmán, following a well-worn trail, headed home: to the mountains of Sinaloa.

Crackberry

Wherever information gathers and flows, two predators follow closely behind it: censorship and surveillance.

—Sarah Jeong, writing in *The Atlantic*, April 2016

FIVE

The Office

February 2012–October 2012

With helicopters hovering and an army of policemen on his tail, Chapo Guzmán was a fugitive again. After getting off the beach in Punta Ballena, he made his way to a car and hurried north, moving up the Transpeninsular Highway to an airstrip in La Paz where his bodyguard Condor had arranged a private plane. Whatever had just happened, it must have been a disconcerting wakeup call. Not since his arrest in 1993 had the authorities—let alone the *gringo* authorities— come so close to catching him. As he later told his wife, he had seen them coming at the final moment and rushed out the back door of the mansion, sprinting past his swimming pool and leaping over the low wall of his deck. He had left the house so fast there had been no time to grab his laptop, his address book, even his underwear.

10:00 P.M.: I saw them pounding on the door next door and I was able to jump out. . . .

10:01 P.M.: Oh love, that's horrible.

When he got back to Culiacán that night and moved into a safe house on a quiet street in the seedy neighborhood of Colonia Libertad, Guzmán did his usual postmortem. Losing the address book was bad, but losing the laptop was considerably worse. The computer's files contained his FlexiSPY accounts, and as the days went by, he began to worry that whoever had it now could search his browser history and find them. In the interests of security, he asked one of his tech chiefs, Charly Martinez, to reach out to the young Colombian, Christian Rodriguez, who had set the system up, and have him change the passwords. While it might have been a wiser course to have gotten rid of the program altogether, Guzmán was eager to know who had betrayed him in Los Cabos. It could easily have been one of his own people, and if that was the case, then he could not afford to shut the spyware down.

What he did shut down were Rodriguez's secret cell phones. Not long after settling into Culiacán, Guzmán issued an order to his staff: from here on, he announced, everyone around him was going to work exclusively on BlackBerries. The encrypted Nokias had fallen out of his favor, and by that point he had largely moved to BlackBerries himself. Many of his closest aides, and all of his wives and girlfriends, were also using BlackBerries by then—the ones infected with the FlexiSPY malware. The abrupt change in methods did not appear, at least at first, to suggest a lack of trust in Christian Rodriguez. Rather, Guzmán seems to have believed that BlackBerries were simply more secure than other available devices, and after the breach in Cabo, he needed more security.

Many drug traffickers were under that impression. There was a general consensus at the time that BlackBerry's chatting service, BBM, offered more protections than competing texting apps: the system's messages moved phone to phone not by way of ordinary numbers, but instead by way of mostly anonymous alphanumeric PINs. It was also common knowledge—at least to those who made a point of knowing—that the company's servers were in Canada, safe from the eyes and ears of the American federal government. BlackBerry users could purchase special add-ons from outside firms that enhanced the device's normal safeguards. One of them, Phantom Secure, customized off-the-shelf handsets with additional encryption and routed BBM chats through servers in Panama and Hong Kong, places that were famously unhelpful to law enforcement agents.

There was only one drawback to the BlackBerries: their native encryption system was much less robust than the one the Nokias had. To compensate for this, Guzmán put in place a clever new method of protecting himself against the menace of surveillance. Moving forward, he decided, his organization's BBM chats would not be sent directly from one phone to another; instead they would be channeled through a kind of message web, a network of filters he came to call the Office.[17]

As he envisioned it, the Office would be shaped like a pyramid. At its lowest, fattest level were his operatives in the field: everyone from pilots in Ecuador to couriers in Phoenix. To send the boss a message, the field-level workers would pass it up to a first tier of go-betweens using BlackBerries with screen names like Ofis-1 or Ofis-2. These ten or so Ofis-level workers would then take screen shots of the messages or copy them by hand and push them on to a second tier of filters; they had devices screen-named Telcel and Usacel. The Telcel-level workers would forward the messages further up the chain—this time, to Condor, Guzmán's bodyguard, or to Condor's partner, another former soldier called Chaneke. At the top of pyramid, Condor and Chaneke (pronounced *chah-NECK-ay*) would deliver the messages to Guzmán himself. He could then send comments or responses in the opposite direction on the same circuitous path.

---

17. It is not publicly known if Guzmán himself devised the Office system or if one of his employees dreamed it up and he, as the chief executive, merely implemented it.

When Guzmán established the Office in the early months of 2012, one of his first steps was to set up what amounted to call centers for his Ofis- and Telcel-level workers. In the call centers, his beleaguered cutouts gorged themselves on junk food and worked around the clock on arrays of numbered BlackBerries, relaying messages up and down the pyramid. The centers were often housed in ordinary homes in ordinary neighborhoods of ordinary cities; the earliest seem to have been based in Tepic, just south of Sinaloa. Imagine General Motors installing an army of assistants in an apartment in Topeka and ordering them to transcribe the emails of the company's top executives all day long, seven days a week, and then to pass their notes on to a second group of similar assistants. From the outside, the call centers didn't look like much; but from within, they were furious hives, serving as the switchboard for Guzmán's sprawling empire.

With the Office up and running, Guzmán returned to work that spring with a kind of refreshed ferocity. As the shock of Cabo started to recede, his business stabilized and his interests were as various as ever. His staple product—Colombian cocaine—was still arriving by the ton-load from suppliers in the country, helped along by trans-shipment teams working out of cattle ranches and melon farms in Honduras and Guatemala. His marijuana profits had slipped in recent years, but bales of pot continued to come down to him from loyal farmers based in the Sierras. Though Jorge Cifuentes had fled to Venezuela after his indictment, Guzmán maintained his project in Ecuador, changing some key players but keeping the smuggling route more or less intact. His border teams, meanwhile, were making frequent crossings at Nogales, Agua Prieta and Ciudad Juárez, despite the war that had been raging there for years.

A central focus of his efforts at the time was building up his operations in Canada. While Guzmán had been shipping drugs to Canada since at least 2008, its busy cities, wide expanses and open border with the United States had persuaded him that there was room for growth. It hadn't gone unnoticed that a kilo of cocaine sold for almost ten thousand dollars more in Montreal and Toronto than it did in Chicago or Los Angeles. In Cabo, Alex Cifuentes, whose ex-wife was Canadian, had introduced Guzmán to a few potential customers from Canada. When they were back in Culiacán, Alex began arranging more meetings about deals in the country in Guzmán's house in Colonia Libertad.

Among those who met with the kingpin was Stephen Tello, a thirtysomething real-estate agent from Toronto. After dropping out of college, Tello, who was of Colombian descent, had bounced around through jobs in finance and precious metals, but ultimately landed in the drug trade, for which he had a talent. With Alex acting as their translator, Tello and Guzmán soon reached an agreement. The kingpin's people—supervised by Damaso López—would ferry loads of cocaine and methamphetamine across the Mexican border to warehouses in Los Angeles. From there, one of Tello's men—a truck fleet owner nicknamed Russian Mike—would move the product up the West Coast in tractor-trailers equipped with secret compartments. When the drugs reached Canada, they would fall back under Alex's supervision. Guzmán now considered Canada to be of such importance to his larger operation that he sent one of his nephews, Mario, there to serve as his man on the ground.

The route in Canada took off like a rocket. In due course, shipments of cocaine were being flown by helicopter from bases in Seattle to isolated ranches near Vancouver; other loads made their way east to Montreal under the protection of the Hells Angels and were sold on the streets by the Rizzuto crime family, the city's top Mafia group. Greek grocers got involved and, eventually, a crew of Iranian gangsters. The excitement of exploiting a new market seemed to spark Guzmán's creativity. Soon there were discussions about flying merchandise to

Canada on seaplanes, driving it over Lake Champlain on speedboats from Vermont and dropping it into the countryside on GPS-guided parachutes.[18]

That same spring, in search of further conquests, Guzmán turned his attention to one of his oldest pastimes: expanding his holdings at the border. He had always had a sixth sense for detecting weakness in competitors and scanning the horizon he now saw an opening in Nuevo Laredo, the bustling border town south of Texas controlled by his longtime enemies, the Zetas.

The Zetas were a unique phenomenon of the drug trade in Mexico. Their founders had started their careers as professional soldiers, serving in an airborne Special Forces unit called the GAFE, or the Grupo Aeromovil de Fuerzas Especiales. Highly trained in counterinsurgency and small-arms tactics, they were deployed for a time in the brutal fight *against* the country's drug cartels. In the late 1990s, however, a handful of the soldiers were lured from the military by Osiel Cárdenas, the erstwhile boss of the Gulf Cartel, to work as his private army and to help him keep control of his organization and its base in Nuevo Laredo. When Cárdenas was arrested in 2003, the Zetas started to strike out on their own, taking over his smuggling routes and moving into ancillary rackets like kidnapping and extortion. The infighting and instability this created caught Guzmán's eye. That same year, drafting his own private army, Los Negros—or the Black Ones—the kingpin launched his first invasion of Nuevo

---

18. In a further sign of just how booming business in Canada was, within a matter of months, Andrea Velez started dating Stephen Tello. Andrea traveled frequently to Canada on Alex's behalf and her romance with Tello blossomed during the visits. Alex was displeased by the relationship, largely because Tello had recently been divorced. He ordered Andrea to end it, telling her, apparently without irony, that she needed to show good morals. "These are not normal people," Andrea said.

Laredo. But the Zetas proved too much for him and he eventually retreated.

Nine years later, not much had changed. In March 2012, even as the kingpin was setting up his new Canadian business, a convoy of soldiers stormed Nuevo Laredo in a deliberate assault against the Zetas' boss in the city, Gerardo Guerra-Valdez. A skilled tactician, Guerra-Valdez responded by blockading roads near the World Trade Bridge and surprised his attackers with a fusillade of rocket-propelled grenades. In the wild gunfight that ensued, Guerra-Valdez was killed with two other top Zeta commanders. On its surface, this was the commonest sort of drug war violence, with one important difference: Nuevo Laredo, a strategic crossing with a pliant police force and easy highway access to Houston, Dallas and all points east, was now essentially leaderless. Seizing the moment, Guzmán moved in.

Once again, the kingpin conscripted a surrogate militia. This time, it was a hit squad called the Matazetas, or the Zeta Killers, which had recently emerged from within a rising powerhouse, the New Generation Jalisco Cartel. Run by an upstart named Nemesio Oseguera, aka El Mencho, the Matazetas were exceptionally brutal even by Mexican standards. When the fighting broke out, in a second war in April, it was short-lived but appalling. Over three brief months, Guzmán's deputized assassins hung their dead from bridges, set off car bombs and dismembered scores of victims. In one attack, fourteen headless bodies were discovered in a car near the local Customs office. The heads were elsewhere: stuffed in plastic coolers in front of City Hall.

As Guzmán took control of Nuevo Laredo, there were problems at the call centers.

Toward the end of June, the Mexican police launched an unexpected raid on one of his facilities in Tepic and four young men from Culiacán, sitting in front of a tableful of BlackBerries, were arrested.

When the kingpin was informed about the raid, he immediately tossed out two of his own BlackBerries and seized three more from his wives and girlfriends, tossing them as well. His cutouts at the call center had been handling the messages flowing back and forth and he feared that the devices had been compromised.

Three days later, despite these precautions, the police broke into his other call center in Tepic. Two more Culichis—with two more BlackBerries—were detained.

Something seemed to be going on. In less than a week both his Ofis-level workers and his Telcel team had been taken into custody, and Guzmán fretted about what it all might mean. The arrests in Tepic had come only four months after his own close brush with capture in Los Cabos. But what was the connection? *Was* there a connection? Just as he was struggling to piece things together, one of his girlfriends in Culiacán—she, too, had a BlackBerry—nervously got word to him that she was being followed by what may have been Americans. Something was definitely going on. But what?

It remains unclear exactly how Guzmán figured it out, but after the incidents in Cabo, Tepic and Culiacán, he must have triangulated his suspicions and come to the conclusion that there was a mole inside his organization. Though he didn't grasp the full extent of the emergency— and didn't know that Marston and Potash, still on his trail, had sent the police to Tepic—he nearly sniffed them out. Guzmán reasoned that the culprit could only be one person: the young man who had access to his BlackBerries through FlexiSPY, Christian Rodriguez.[19]

---

19. After losing Guzmán in Los Cabos, Marston and Potash had been able to leverage FlexiSPY to identify the PINs for a handful of new BlackBerries the kingpin was using. With these PINs, they were able to generate what they believed were locational coordinates for Guzmán in Tepic. But they did not know about the Office system yet and did not realize that the BlackBerries they were tracking were not in fact in Guzmán's hands, but were instead cutouts in a call center, mirroring the messages that the kingpin was sending and receiving.

Security being paramount, Guzmán shut the spyware system down for good that summer, then sought to do the same to the traitor who had installed it, placing a contract on Rodriguez's head. As he often did with sensitive tasks, he gave the job of dealing with the young technician to his old friend Alex Cifuentes; as Alex often did himself, he passed it on to his assistant Andrea.

In August 2012, Andrea was sent to Medellín on a mission to find Rodriguez and lure him back to Mexico. By that point, she had been working for Alex and Guzmán for nearly four years and had traveled the world for them, acting as their avatar in meetings with film producers, corrupt army officers and Montreal mobsters. She had moved their money, vetted their customers and helped them purchase airplanes. But leading a man to his certain death, especially an innocent and a fellow Colombian like Rodriguez, was a line she wouldn't cross.

Touching down in Medellín, Andrea sent word to the technician through two of her girlfriends that his life was in danger and he needed to leave the country quickly. After a day or two, she stalled for time and reported back to Alex and Guzmán that even though she had searched for Rodriguez on Facebook and Google, she was not able to find him. When the two men pressed her for a lead, Andrea took another grave risk. She gave her bosses a false address, hoping she could throw them off the trail.

Even if the address had been real, Guzmán's killers would not have found their target. Around the time Andrea arrived in Medellín, Alex reached out to his mother in Colombia to warn her that Rodriguez was a turncoat and to let her know that the Spark, the encrypted system he had built for their family, could no longer be trusted. But his admonition, far more prescient than he realized, had come too late. Rodriguez still had access to the family's servers, and he ultimately listened to the call in which Alex told his mother that it had been "confirmed one hundred percent" that the young technician was an American spy.

Logging off in a panic, Rodriguez called Bob Potash. He was gone within hours, fleeing to safety in the United States.

To anyone who understood how Guzmán and his crew conducted business, it would not have been surprising to have learned that an assassination plot had gone awry when the man in charge of it accidentally revealed its existence in a phone call to his mother. Despite its reputation for efficiency, the kingpin's operation was not always the crack criminal enterprise it was assumed to be. Though Guzmán was savvy, he was also reckless, hindered by his own self-absorption and a circle of allies and underlings who were prone to missteps that might have seemed hilarious if they had taken place in a different, less deadly line of business. Alex Cifuentes was often the principal offender in this respect, but he was not the only one. His older brother, Jorge, was a pathological cheat who once shoved a helicopter off a cliff to collect the insurance. One of Guzmán's early mentors, Juan José Esparragoza, nearly killed the organization's entire senior leadership one day by misfiring a bazooka. Cholo Ivan Gastelum, the group's enforcer in Los Mochis, was in debt to his local gas station, and two of its workers in Honduras almost died while foolishly standing on an airstrip as an inbound drug flight veered off course on landing. Guzmán's sons, meanwhile—especially his eldest, Iván Archivaldo—were feckless ne'er-do-wells with a taste for gaudy nightclubs and their own cocaine. When Iván was arrested in his early twenties—his release sparked the war with Arturo Beltran-Leyva—he underwent a psychological evaluation. The prison analyst found that he lacked impulse control and had a tendency to channel his aggression into the domination of those he felt were beneath him. At the same time, when he was asked to fill in the blank following the phrase *I wish my father*, Iván wrote: ". . . was with me."

It might have been expected that after the events in Cabo, Guzmán would have gone to ground, cutting off unnecessary contacts and lying low until the heat of the moment passed. That he did neither—pushing instead into Canada, launching a new war of expansion and carrying on like always with his lovers—suggests both his arrogance and carelessness. If personal security had always been his primary concern, ego and publicity were never far behind. Within ten days of the Cabo raid, *Forbes* magazine had placed the kingpin on its annual list of billionaires for the fourth year in a row. (Baseball caps were available on eBay emblazoned with the number 701, his initial ranking on the list.) Five days later, thousands of people flocked to the website *El Blog del Narco* to watch a bootleg video of Guzmán questioning a suspected spy at Damaso López's ranch. That same week, in March 2012, Marston and Potash, still collecting FlexiSPY texts, caught the kingpin swapping BBM chats with one of his younger mistresses. The two were making plans for Guzmán to withdraw some of his sperm from a cold storage bank in Guadalajara so that she could be inseminated at a fertility clinic in Culiacán.

He had even returned to the enduring fantasy of making his movie. Though Guzmán had just evaded capture by the FBI and the DEA, he invited his biographer, Javier Rey, to his safe house in Colonia Libertad to conduct more interviews for the *El Padrino* manuscript. Their deal by then was nearly on the ropes. Having secured the rights to Guzmán's story, Rey had unwisely tried to strong-arm his subject into giving up thirty-five percent of the project's profits. Guzmán, insulted, began to suspect that Rey was an informant. When the writer left Culiacán, the kingpin hatched a plot to lure Rey to his death with the promise of a quick advance payment. In a rare burst of scruples, Alex Cifuentes ultimately warned Rey of the plan.

By that point, however, the kingpin no longer needed a writer. He had turned his gaze toward a bigger prize: the Mexican soap opera star

Kate del Castillo. Guzmán had been obsessed with del Castillo ever since he'd watched her performance in *The Queen of the South,* a telenovela from 2011 in which she had played his old friend the real-life drug queen Sandra Ávila Beltran. Vacationing in Cabo, he was even more enthralled when del Castillo sat at her computer one night and wrote on Twitter: "Today I believe more in El Chapo Guzmán than I do in the governments that hide truths from me. . . . MR. CHAPO, WOULDN'T IT BE COOL IF YOU STARTED TRAFFICKING WITH THE GOOD? . . . COME ON, SEÑOR, YOU WOULD BE THE HERO OF HEROES."

The invitation, though absurd, closely synced with Guzmán's own self-image. As soon as he got out of Cabo, he ordered Alex to get in touch with del Castillo.

All of this was taking place against the larger backdrop of a Mexican election that stood to have a decisive impact on Guzmán and his business. After six years as president, Felipe Calderón had been barred by term limits from running again, and the three-way race to pick his successor—scheduled for July 2012—was, not surprisingly, a referendum on the most important policy of his time in office: his all-out war on Mexico's cartels. While Calderón's predecessor, Vicente Fox, had also taken a tough stance toward the traffickers, the outbound president had put the fight on steroids. From the moment he took power, in late 2006, Calderón announced that the military would assume control of subduing the country's narcos. Within a year thousands of troops were deployed across Mexico on heavy-handed antidrug maneuvers. Ski-masked soldiers patrolled the streets from Michoacán to Baja California. Army half-tracks were posted in front of police stations. Big cities and small towns alike began to look like villages in occupied Iraq.

Calderón's crackdown had some notable successes. Under his watch, the military had killed or captured several cartel leaders—chief among them Guzmán's longtime enemy, Arturo Beltran-Leyva. But the offensive ultimately led to as many as sixty thousand deaths and left much of Mexico psychically battered and exhausted. In searching for a militarized solution to the violence, Calderón not only under-estimated his adversaries' capacity for mayhem; he mistook the traf-fickers as an external threat to the Mexican establishment instead of seeing them and the establishment as inextricably linked. By sending troops into his own despondent cities, he also managed to impose the terrors of state repression on the same population he had promised to protect.

From the start of his *sexenio*, Calderón never fully grasped how deeply the financial health and welfare of his country were tied to narco-trafficking. By 2009, his third year in office, Mexico's gangsters were taking in an estimated thirty billion dollars a year, second only to the total earnings of the national oil industry. Much of that money was injected back in the economy through follow-on payments to farmers, drivers, couriers, security guards, restaurant owners, real-estate agents and auto salesmen—not to mention bankers who quietly laundered untold millions in cartel profits. Calderón may have be-lieved that he was fighting organized crime by pressing his campaign against Guzmán and his colleagues. But given the complicity of tens of thousands of ordinary people in the system, he was really fighting a bloc of his own constituents.

Predictably, all three candidates who were seeking to replace him wanted nothing to do with this morass. Each of them—including the eventual winner, Enrique Peña Nieto—had vowed in their campaigns to refocus the drug war, but all were short on details as to how they might accomplish that or exactly what it meant. Peña Nieto, a hand-some former governor with a sunny disposition and a glamorous second wife, ran on a slogan of *"Tu Me Conoces"*—"You Know Me"—despite the fact that all that most people knew was that he had a gift for making speeches and had been born into a family with deep connections to the Institutional Revolutionary Party, or the PRI. After running Mexico for most of the twentieth century, the PRI had been booted out of office in 2000 by Vicente Fox, not the least because it had a history of corruption and had managed the country for decades in a kind of power-sharing arrangement with the traffickers. During his campaign, Peña Nieto made the anodyne promise to spend less time and money chasing gangsters and more of both fighting the violence that had devastated ordinary Mexicans. His opponents attacked him and the PRI for appeasing the cartels and for wanting to restore their old agreements with the drug lords. While Peña Nieto angrily denied these allegations, refuting them even in his victory speech, the irony was that they might not have hurt him all that badly. By the time of the elections that summer, despair and weariness with the drug war had reached such desperate levels that many in Mexico didn't seem to mind if their incoming president had reached a new *acuerdo* with the mafia. Provided, of course, that a respite from the bloodshed was included in the deal.

Guzmán wasn't interested in the particulars of politics, but he had always been attuned to the ebbs and flows of political power. A few months after the election, he pulled Alex Cifuentes aside and told him about an intriguing message he said he had received from an unnamed source who was close to Peña Nieto. According to Alex, the source had advised the kingpin that the new administration—due to take office in December 2012—knew where he was hiding. In fact, it had a photograph of him from as recently as a few days before. But the president-elect, it was explained, saw no reason why Guzmán should have to continue living on the run—if an accommodation could be reached. In Alex's account, the source put the price of that accommodation at two hundred fifty million dollars.

Peña Nieto has repeatedly denied that he sought a bribe from Guzmán and in assessing the veracity of the charge, it should be noted
that Damaso López, who knew more than anyone about the kingpin's operations, claims he never heard of such a thing. ("It is a lot of
money," Damaso later said.) It is also the case that Alex Cifuentes—
the only man to have discussed the allegation in public—is a serial
liar who cannot be trusted blindly.

Still, as far-fetched as it sounded, Alex had heard something
vaguely corroborative from his assistant Andrea Velez. During the
elections, Andrea was still working with J. J. Rendón, the political
consultant who had helped to run the Peña Nieto campaign.
Rendón, known for collecting samurai swords and bingeing on
espresso, is a right-wing strategist who has often used his roguish
brilliance to aid conservative candidates. Not long after Peña Nieto's victory in July, Andrea sent Alex a cell-phone photo of a suitcase
filled with cash lying around in one of Rendón's offices in Mexico
City. She has since said that she isn't sure precisely how the money
got there. But she has also said that she knows where it came from:
her other employer, Chapo Guzmán. A few days before the case
appeared in Rendón's office, Andrea herself had given it to Guzmán
during one of her routine money runs. The cash inside, she said,
was still packaged in the cartel's signature fashion: with twenty-
dollar bills collected into rubber-banded bundles of two thousand
dollars.

Andrea considered the whole thing to be strange, but she remains
adamant that Rendón had nothing to do with funneling cash from
Guzmán to Peña Nieto. (Rendón himself has vociferously denied the
accusation.) "J. J. can be crazy," Andrea said. "But I've never seen him
receive money from narcos. And I was very close to him."

For his own part, Alex Cifuentes claims that Guzmán never did in
fact give Peña Nieto or anyone around him two hundred fifty million
dollars; instead, he managed to negotiate the payment down to a

hundred million dollars. Even that sum, Alex recalled the kingpin saying, had required a large and difficult increase in revenue—just the sort of thing that extra shipments to Canada and a lucrative new smuggling route through Nuevo Laredo might provide.

SIX

The Coalition

When Special Agent Ray Donovan arrived for his first day of work at the DEA's Special Operations Division, walking into a drab government building in an office park in Chantilly, Virginia, he found the men and women who would soon become his partners in chasing Chapo Guzmán still chewing over the FBI's huge missed opportunity in Cabo San Lucas. It was early September 2012, a little more than six months after the kingpin slipped away. As Donovan discovered, SOD's assessment of Operation Server Jack was that it was a shitshow.

Methodologically, he heard his colleagues say, the mission had been brilliant: pure technical genius. But from a management perspective? Shitshow. For months, the watercooler grousers said, the bureau's case agents, acting more like spies than cops, had simply listened as the world's most famous drug lord went about his business. Even after the DEA had launched its own raids in Cabo, the FBI, they felt, had been disinclined to share intelligence. If the raids had been a shitshow too, the general consensus at SOD was still that the bureau could have—and should have—acted sooner. "They weren't nullifying the target—they were sitting on his phone," said Donovan's new supervisor in the unit's Mexican section. "It was frustrating to think there was a branch of government that was up on Guzmán for more than a year. If we'd had their information at the time, we could have taken him off the streets."

In his new position as a staff coordinator, Donovan's job at SOD was to bring federal agencies together, not divide them further. While he, too, may have looked askance at Server Jack's go-it-alone administrative style, he preferred—as the unit's new guy—to focus on the future. Founded in 1992, SOD was created to serve as that rarest of governmental entities: a centralized hub of information. Under the motto "One Team, One Fight," its investigators not only funded and supported operations in dozens of DEA offices around the world; they also tried to build bridges to other US law enforcement outfits and to the intelligence community. Within a week of arriving at the division's headquarters on the outskirts of Dulles Airport, Donovan went to see the unit's leader, Derek Maltz, with an ambitious game plan squarely in keeping with its interagency mandate.

"I want to be a part of something that's going after Chapo," Donovan said.

"I love your attitude, kid," Maltz answered with a laugh.

But Donovan was serious.

"We'll put something together," he promised—not by accident in the first-person plural. "We'll figure out how to get him."

That first week, Donovan dove in to the biggest homework assignment of his career, poring over everything that SOD had gathered on Guzmán and the Sinaloa drug cartel. Sitting at his desk for hours at a stretch, he turned the pages of investigative and intelligence reports, absorbing the kingpin's expansive history and the seemingly unending attempts to capture him over the years. Born in the Bronx to a single mother who raised five children and worked three jobs, Donovan approached this task hardwired with an almost manic sense of tenacity. When he first joined the DEA in 1998 as a member of a task force in New York—a team of federal agents, city detectives and local state troopers—he quickly earned a reputation as a first-in, last-out kind of guy. In one of his early cases, Donovan developed an informant in the Bronx who tipped him off that a warehouse in the Hunts Point food market was being used to stash cocaine. Setting up surveillance, he watched the building on a live feed from his office every day for nine months straight, sometimes until two in the morning. At just the point where most of his task-force buddies thought he was insane, a tractor-trailer turned down Hunts Point Avenue and backed into the warehouse's cargo bay. The bust that resulted was relatively small: a little more than three hundred kilos. But where other agents might have made the collar and taken the statistics, Donovan and his colleagues traced the truck back to its origins, squeezing sources and tracking leads through Mexico to Colombia then all the way to Panama. Two years later, their labors paid off with a bigger bust—this time, of a Panamanian merchant freighter linked to Guzmán's ally-turned-enemy, Arturo Beltran-Leyva. The ship was carrying nearly twenty thousand kilos of cocaine—or almost twenty tons. It was, at the time, the largest drug seizure in DEA history.

One of Donovan's specialties was digging into the communication networks of vast drug mafias and leveraging wiretaps to piece together detailed maps of who was who within the organizations. It was a skill that served him well as he spent months acclimating himself to the disorienting world of live investigations into Guzmán. By late 2012, there were dozens of active cases—in New York, Chicago, Miami, El Paso and as far away as Spain and China—that touched at least in part on the kingpin and his empire. Many of these efforts, Donovan determined, could trace their roots to a landmark wire investigation that had started in Los Angeles that spring.

Coming up for air one night, Donovan realized something. The DEA already had everything it needed to go after Chapo Guzmán, but the tips and tools were scattered in the files of scores of different agents strewn across the country. A vast amount of investigative energy had been lavished on the kingpin in the past three years, and yet there was no single effort or overarching strategy to track him down and capture him. It was, Donovan felt, the usual governmental siloing. Separate offices in separate cities were all laying hands, like blind men, on different parts of the giant Guzmán elephant.

But what if—and he knew it was a big if—they could come together and hunt the elephant as a team?

Looking for a way to build that team, Donovan immersed himself in the mother case from Los Angeles: Operation Crackberry.

Like many breakthrough investigations, Crackberry started with an innocuous event. In May 2012, just before Donovan arrived at SOD, a Mexican money courier was picked up during a traffic stop in Beverly Hills. Under questioning, the courier admitted that the five hundred thousand dollars in cash discovered in his car belonged to the Sinaloa drug cartel. He also coughed up a fascinating tip: his own connection to the organization—Heriberto Zazueta-Godoy—had been keeping in touch with him and the rest of the cartel through BlackBerry Messenger, or BBM, BlackBerry's proprietary chatting service. Zazueta-Godoy, better known as Capi Beto, was a big fish in Sinaloa's corporate structure, a top logistics expert for Guzmán and Mayo Zambada responsible for moving huge loads of cocaine from Central America through Mexico and then across the border. Donovan already had his own strange link to Capi Beto. Years before, the transport specialist had helped to plan the twenty-ton shipment from Panama that Donovan had busted early in his career.

The LA office of the DEA immediately opened a case on Capi Beto, hoping to follow his trail of BBM chats back to his bosses in Mexico. But when the agents started looking for the legal means to tap into his BlackBerry, they ran into a curious dead end. Anyone, it seemed, could send a BlackBerry chat to anyone else from anywhere in the world. But no matter where the chats originated, BlackBerry routed them through its own internal relay servers in Canada. Because the servers were not in the United States, they were technically beyond the reach of American surveillance. In June 2012, however, just as the LA case seemed doomed to fail, the agents got an unexpected gift: BlackBerry's parent company, Research in Motion, suddenly relocated its servers from Canada to Texas. That single, fortuitous decision put Capi Beto—and his BBM chats—back within the crosshairs of the California office.

A wiretap was approved on Capi Beto and in almost no time it was spewing like a fire hose. Within a matter of weeks, the agents in LA were drowning in information. Their line sheets were endless and each passing day contained new chats about pickup times, drop-off times, load sizes, warehouse locations, the names of couriers, the phone numbers for drivers, even Facebook links to news reports of seizures. The LA office could barely keep up. Capi Beto, a major player, was hooked into deals all over the world, and as he thumbed his BBMs to operatives from Ecuador to Ohio, each new BlackBerry he contacted was also subject to the tap. Soon, the web of targets expanded exponentially and the agents in LA were forced to farm out leads to colleagues in twenty-one domestic offices and nineteen foreign offices—all of them eavesdropping on Sinaloa BlackBerries. It was as if the cartel's collective brain had suddenly grown a voice.

"It was a feeding frenzy," said Wayne Rositano, one of Donovan's partners at SOD. "It seemed too good to be true."

To Donovan, Crackberry was a game changer. The direct results of the operation were notable on their own: a steady drumbeat of busts and arrests around the world. But more important, Crackberry transformed the way that the DEA conducted surveillance, especially in Mexico. Before the operation, federal agents depended on the Mexican authorities to tap communications devices being used inside their country. If their cooperation was not forthcoming (which it often was not) or was hindered by corruption (which it often was), the DEA was forced to build its cases the old-fashioned way: a laborious process of making seizures, arresting suspects and trying to turn them into informants. Now, however, if BlackBerries were being used—and increasingly they were, as Capi Beto had shown—the agency could run its own wiretaps on foreign subjects straight from American soil.

"Prior to Crackberry, we were in the dark," Donovan said. "But once we had the new technique, it opened everything up. It was like an explosion. Stuff started coming in from everywhere."

The technology that Crackberry unleashed became a kind of investigative accelerant. When the ability to wiretap BBM chats was applied to cases that were already smoldering, they erupted into flames.

For arcane legal reasons, the agents in LA had initially used state law to authorize their wire. By the end of the year, however, their investigation into Capi Beto and his crew had become so complicated they needed a federal partner. After an aborted courtship in their own backyard, they chose to work with the United States attorney's office in Chicago. It was a logical decision. By late 2012, the Chicago office—or in federal parlance, the Northern District of Illinois—was three years into one of the most robust Sinaloa prosecutions in the country. The case had at first been based on cartel turncoats. Pedro and Margarito Flores, the Chicago-born twins who handled much of Guzmán's American distribution, had by that time reached a plea agreement in northern Illinois and provided prosecutors in the office with a trove of secretly recorded audiotapes of Guzmán and his minions committing various drug deals. Handsome, charismatic and born speaking English, the twins were poised to be devastating witnesses if the crime lord was ever put on trial. The story they could tell was both damning and meticulously detailed. In the broadest sense, the brothers could describe selling as much as forty tons of Guzmán's cocaine over the years, earning him a staggering fortune of nearly a billion dollars. On the micro level, they could talk about his neurotic demand that they send their profits back to him in hundred-dollar bills, not the tens and twenties they collected from the streets. Larger denominations, they were told, were easier to count.

Chicago had another, perhaps even better, star witness queued up: Vicente Zambada, the son of Mayo Zambada, Guzmán's longtime partner. Not yet forty, Vicente had been groomed since childhood to serve as the cartel's heir apparent, a child of royalty anointed to run the Sinaloa kingdom when Guzmán and Mayo retired. In 2009, however, this succession plan had been interrupted when Vicente was arrested by troops in Mexico City and was shipped to Chicago to stand trial. There, he dropped a bombshell while fighting his prosecution. The cartel princeling claimed that just before he was taken into custody, he had met with a group of American officials and reached a secret deal with them to trade information on Sinaloa's rivals in exchange for permission to run his business freely. While it was certainly the case that Vicente had spoken with the DEA and Chicago federal prosecutors under cloak-and-dagger circumstances in a Mexican hotel room, the American authorities denied a quid pro quo. When a judge agreed, Vicente was stripped of his best defense and decided to cooperate with the office in Chicago—right about the time it inherited the Crackberry wire from Los Angeles. The combination of Vicente's human intelligence and Crackberry's eavesdropping technology produced one of Donovan's explosions. Chicago was soon tapped into the deepest levels of Guzmán's organization, grabbing BlackBerry chats not only from Capi Beto, but also from one of the kingpin's sons, from his chief of staff and from a top cartel assassin.

Something similar was taking place in San Diego. In June 2012, the same month Crackberry was launched, the police in Chula Vista, California, stopped a man named Hector Larranga for pausing at a red light with his front tires illegally touching a crosswalk. In the trunk of his car were four bricks of cocaine neatly packed in gift wrap. The Larranga case appeared at first to be a modest step in a modest probe of a modest distribution ring based in the suburbs of San Diego County. But in mid-December, after some of the suspects were found to be using BlackBerry Messenger, the DEA's San Diego office went up on a wiretap in an operation code-named Narco Polo. The Narco Polo wire and the Chicago wire were soon joined at the hip and as the taps progressed, they focused on a new and growing list of targets. In San Diego, those included another one of Guzmán's sons; three more of Mayo's sons; Guzmán's top man in Culiacán, his stronghold city near the mountains; and a few key leaders of the two men's favorite hit team, a band of killers who called themselves Los Antrax.

As the winter went on, so did the roaring Crackberry wildfire. In early 2013, it spread to Arizona, where a group of agents from a little-known law enforcement outfit, Homeland Security Investigations (HSI), working from a small regional office near the border in Nogales, went up on what was now a third BlackBerry wire. The Homeland Security case—Operation Paisano—had started two years earlier as a domestic undercover probe targeting a money-laundering ring that was making cash drops everywhere from shopping malls in Atlanta to public sidewalks in New York. When the agents discovered that some of the money launderers were using BBM, the investigation pivoted midstream. Using the new tool that Crackberry provided, they followed a heavy flow of BlackBerry chats from the money movers to a cell of transportation experts who were putting together large loads of cocaine in Colombia, Ecuador and Guatemala.

The Arizona border mucks, as they self-effacingly called themselves, were not traditional drug cops like their DEA colleagues in Chicago and San Diego. And while they had not initially set out to join the chase for Guzmán, they were quickly at the heart of it. Their lead agent, Jake Healy, a novice investigator, was, in the way of rookies, already obsessed with one of his first targets: a cartel operative nicknamed Speedy who was sending hundreds of kilos of cocaine from his base in Guatemala back to his masters in Mexico. As Speedy went about his business, he never stopped texting, knocking out as many as a thousand BBMs a day. Sitting in Nogales, Healy was mystified by Speedy's constant chatter. Moreover, no one seemed to have a clue about who he was: there was nothing on him in any of the usual federal databases. In his office and at home over beers, Healy read and reread Speedy's line sheets, wondering who this industrious motormouth could be.

The problem was that the wiretap on Speedy—like those in all the other cities—was busy, dense and maddeningly baffling. The coded messages, coming in around the clock, were practically inscrutable:

11:14 P.M.: Good evening, buddy. We need to send MEMO to unit 10 and my friend from MEXICO just checked in. He says the RATS are bewildered, and they have not heard from the godson at all. On the other hand, buddy, how is POLLITO doing?

11:29 P.M.: Okay, that was good news about your friend. God willing we can continue like that. Very good on the MEMO matter. POLLITO agreed to check in tomorrow, saying he had a meeting with the friend that manufactures the furniture that is imported. He said all was going good.

The people sending these texts were as mysterious as the messages themselves, and dozens of them were now showing up on wiretap lines across the country. Each appeared to be using a secret screen name: Cobra, Jorgon, Hugo Boss. The monikers were much like the ones that Marston and Potash had found in Guzmán's FlexiSPY chats: ornately cryptic, they might—or might not—have been hints at the senders' real identities. Wracking their separate brains in their separate airless wire rooms, the agents in Nogales, San Diego and Chicago had been swiping at this fog for weeks. Juiced on adrenaline and coffee, they were grasping for clues that could help them understand the endless flurry of enigmatic texts.

Who was Enrique? Where was El 19? And what in God's name were the Blue Ones?

This was the bewildering landscape that surrounded Ray Donovan within six months of arriving at SOD. If it wasn't already confusing enough, he had in the meantime inherited his own small piece of the puzzle: yet another wire investigation—Operation Landing Strip—that Special Operations was running with his former colleagues in the DEA's office in New York. Landing Strip, like the case in Arizona, had initially focused on a group of transportation brokers who were buying planes for Guzmán's organization and shopping for him like purchasing agents for sources of cocaine in Central America. But following the now familiar pattern, it turned into a wiretap case that winter when one of the brokers, arrested in Cali, offered up a gem: the BlackBerry PINs for ten of his close associates.

As the New York office started its surveillance, Donovan was excited to discover that these new BlackBerry PINs were all using the same kinds of screen names found on the other BBM wires: Perceo, Biler, Lumbre, Diablo. Donovan became particularly interested

Young Chapo Guzmán, right, out on the town in the late 1980s

Guzmán as an inmate in
Puente Grande prison
in the early 1990s

Unless noted, all photos courtesy of U.S. Attorney's Office in Brooklyn

Guzmán and
Alex Cifuentes in
the mountains of
Sinaloa, Mexico

Guzmán in the mountains with a gold-plated AK-47

Guzmán in one
of his mountain
dance palapas

(Clockwise from top left) Miguel Angel Félix Gallardo, founder of the Guadalajara drug cartel; Ismael "El Mayo" Zambada, Guzmán's longtime partner; Jesus "El Rey" Zambada, Mayo's brother; Damaso López Nuñez, Guzmán's chief of staff

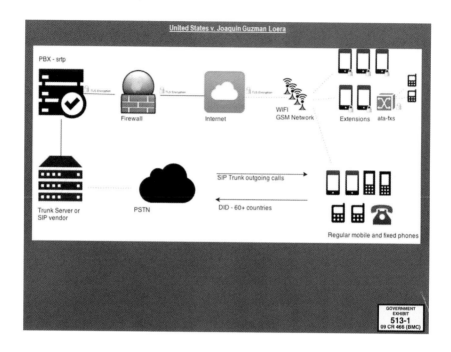

(Above) The visual aide Christian Rodriguez used to demonstrate his encrypted cellphone system to Guzmán

(Left) A view of the footsteps leading from the mansion in Cabo San Lucas from which Guzman escaped a 2012 raid by Mexican and American authorities

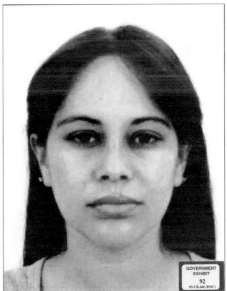

(Left) Emma Coronel Aispuro, Guzmán's current wife
(Right) Lucero Sánchez, Guzmán's mistress

(Above) Guzmán's safe house, the Five, in Culiacán, from which he escaped in a tunnel hidden under a bathtub

(Left) DEA agent Victor Vazquez in Guzmán's tunnel at the Five (photo credit: DEA)

Bathtub tunnel entrance

The Hotel Miramar, in Mazatlán, where Guzmán was captured in a fourth-floor room in February 2014

Guzmán, on a plane, bound for the United States after his extradition in 2017

in Diablo. There were indications that he was extremely close to Guzmán—perhaps was even a member of his family.

The early months of 2013 were unprecedented. Around the country, American federal agents were running no less than four separate wiretaps tracking different aspects of the kingpin's massive Black-Berry network. As the year began, Donovan started reaching out to his colleagues in Chicago, San Diego and Nogales, hoping to connect their efforts to his own in Chantilly and New York. From his first week at SOD, he had dreamed of going after Guzmán as a team. Now he could envision what amounted to a grand coalition.[20]

There was, however, one last piece to put in place. In the DEA's embassy office in Mexico, an aggressive young agent named Andrew Hogan was also tooling around with Sinaloa BlackBerry PINs. Hogan had been in Mexico for less than a year, but had experience pursuing Guzmán's network. In his previous tour of duty, in San Diego, he and his former partner had helped take down one of the kingpin's most prolific money-laundering operations. When Hogan left for Mexico City, the partner, Juan Sandoval, stayed in California. Continuing their work, Sandoval was later able to squeeze Guzmán's personal BlackBerry PIN from a girlfriend at the border, triggering the raids in Cabo San Lucas.

Hogan, like Donovan, was a number junkie. In his office at the embassy, he had built a database of every PIN connected to Guzmán he could find. Some of the PINs had come to him from the scraps of his investigations with Sandoval. Some had been found by the Mexican police in a coded address book and the call logs of other Black-Berries that Guzmán left behind when he hurried out of his mansion

---

20. Remarkably, there was a *fifth* BlackBerry wire running at the same time, but it was not directly targeting Guzmán or his organization. Based in El Paso, it was targeting a remnant cell of Arturo Beltran-Leyva's operation.

in Los Cabos. Still others, pulled off suspects during drug busts in Colombia and Ecuador, had been sent to Hogan by fellow agents who knew about his obsession with the PINs.

When Donovan, rounding out his team-building mission, got in touch with Hogan, he immediately recognized a synergy. Hogan had a trove of BlackBerry PINs, but was only just beginning to understand the full scope of the wider operation. Donovan was starting to connect the disparate threads of that endeavor and could certainly use more PINs to run through the multicity wiretap machine. Slowly, sometimes grudgingly, the coalition he was hoping to create was coming together. Hogan started talking with his colleagues in Nogales and New York. San Diego had already been talking with Chicago. All of them, of course, were talking with Donovan. This was the way that government was supposed to work—but almost never did.

Meanwhile, the intercepts kept coming.

10:23 A.M.: Good morning sir. Your buddy sends his regards. He said that the technicians will wait two days to see how the trip went because they will be leaving today with PROFE and the technicians so they can teach CANUTO how to make 500 and 500. . . . I will talk to the "flour" guy next week. . . .

By early spring Donovan's coalition was in place. The surveillance teams were holding late-night conference calls, and morning emails traveled back and forth among five cities. As the agents debated and discussed their prey, it sparked a kind of chemical reaction: a collective brain, pursuing a collective brain, started to see connections.

In Mexico, two of Hogan's central targets were Cachimba, the pilot who had flown Guzmán to safety after Cabo, and another one of the kingpin's longtime operatives, Isaias Valdez, a pilot and security expert nicknamed Memin.[21] Both of them began showing up on the Homeland Security wire in Nogales. Two of Nogales's chief targets—the chatterbox Speedy and his partner Omega—turned out to be working in Guatemala with Diablo, Donovan's main target. Oftentimes, a target of the wire in Chicago showed up in San Diego. Just as frequently, a San Diego target showed up in Chicago. At one point, the New York wire crossed targets with San Diego *and* Chicago. That target later popped up in the work of both Hogan and Nogales.

"Everything was separate, but related, and all of it was coming in to us at SOD," Donovan said. "We were all sharing intelligence and starting to paint this picture of what the entire cartel looked like, working independently but together. Think about it like a map of the hierarchy. And now it's starting to come into focus."

There was, in fact, a map—just like from Donovan's old days on the task force. It was a constantly changing jigsaw puzzle that showed the Western Hemisphere and was slowly taking shape on a conference table at SOD.

Along its outer edges were name-labeled photos of the operatives who worked at the origins and end points of Guzmán's empire: his suppliers in Colombia, Peru and Venezuela, and his distribution managers in the United States, Canada and Europe. Moving toward the center from the north were the smuggling teams that worked along the US border; moving toward the center from the south were the transit teams in Panama, Honduras, Belize and Guatemala that springboarded his product up from his source countries to Mexico.

---

21. Héctor Takeshima Valenzuela, aka Cachimba, had long been one of Guzmán's favorite pilots, flying missions that included everything from routine drug runs to hair-of-the-chin escapes. Memin had worked for Guzmán since 2004, starting his career as a low-ranking member of the drug lord's security team. He had also held positions as Guzmán's personal secretary and as a bodyguard for his sons.

Closer still to the core were the internal transportation units that ferried drugs through Mexico. Then, in the middle, the bull's-eye: Guzmán himself and his inner circle of aides in Sinaloa.

Building the map was grueling work that required months of trial, error and collaborative effort. No one person or agency could determine the identities of this Dickensian cast of characters, let alone define the roles they played in the organization. Chicago could turn to its cooperating witnesses, Vicente Zambada and the Flores brothers, for advice. New York was getting tips from another cartel turncoat, Vicente's uncle and Mayo's brother Rey Zambada. There were more secret sources feeding information about Guzmán and his businesses to agents in Miami, Mexico City, Mazatlán and Guayaquil.

The wiretap machine was driving the intelligence, however, and in May 2013, it started to unravel the deep structure of Guzmán's BlackBerry system. Hogan had just gotten his hands on a new PIN; it had been found during a series of cocaine busts on Sinaloa speedboats in Ecuador. That same PIN had recently appeared on the Narco Polo wire in San Diego. When Hogan learned that Jake Healy and his colleagues in Nogales—John Zappone and Nick Nordstrom—were also tracking the PIN, he figured that it must be something important. Hogan asked Healy what he and his guys in Arizona knew about the number.

Searching through their wiretap line sheets, the team in Nogales determined that the popular PIN was linked to a BlackBerry account with an unusual screen name: Ofis-5. The name sounded different than the usual run of personal monikers like Mimi, Chemita and Jaguar, and might have been a shortened version of *oficina*, the Spanish word for "office." Ofis-5 also appeared to be sending huge orders for drugs and issuing commands to several other BlackBerries on the network. Most tellingly, when those BlackBerries got their orders and commands, they often acknowledged them by asking Ofis-5 to send their regards to *El Gerente*, the manager, or to *El Señor*, the boss.

As word of Ofis-5 spread through the coalition, it was quickly seen as a significant development. The deferential titles, *El Gerente* and *El Señor*, were almost certainly meant for Guzmán himself and suggested that Ofis-5 was in direct communication with the boss. If whoever was using the Ofis-5 device was also in close proximity to Guzmán, the account might lead to an even bigger prize: the king-pin's physical location.

And yet it wasn't easy to nail down a target's whereabouts with a BlackBerry PIN; the DEA had learned that lesson in Cabo. While the technology had improved somewhat in the year since Victor Vazquez had lost, then found, his little red man, it still wasn't perfect. What you needed most to track a BlackBerry PIN was the device's corresponding phone number. Only phone numbers, not PINs, were registered with cellular providers. And only cellular providers—or people who could access their networks—could ping a number to get locational coordinates. Hogan didn't have a phone number for Ofis-5. Neither did the wire rooms in San Diego or Nogales.

Donovan, however, could get the number. In the aftermath of Operation Crackberry, a member of his team at SOD had cultivated sources inside Research in Motion, BlackBerry's parent company.[22] When these corporate spies were presented with a PIN, they would quietly slip Donovan's man the corresponding phone number. When Donovan got the number for Ofis-5, he sent it on to Hogan in Mexico. Hogan then passed the number to his own secret sources who pinged it through the Mexican telecom system. At the end of this long chain, Hogan got coordinates for Ofis-5. Like the rest of the coalition, he was surprised to find that Ofis-5 was based in Durango.

A large state capital east of Sinaloa, Durango struck everyone as an unlikely place for Guzmán himself to be based. It didn't seem to fit the kingpin's profile. When Guzmán wasn't in the mountains—or

---

22. The SOD agent who worked with Research in Motion was named Lee Lucas.

at getaways like Cabo—he tended to avoid large cities. The one exception was his stronghold, Culiacán. But in Culiacán he was protected by his safe houses, a Praetorian Guard of gunmen and much of the local police.

But just because Ofis-5 was in Durango, it didn't mean the kingpin had to be there. There was mounting evidence that Ofis-5 was a kind of filter device, or what the coalition was now calling a "mirror," that was handling Guzmán's messages at a distance. All of them were thinking of the raids the year before when the Mexican police had stormed into houses in Tepic and arrested several of Guzmán's men banging away on BlackBerries. Could something similar be happening again?

Yes, they decided, it had to be. Durango had become the new Tepic.

Once Ofis-5 was reenvisioned as a cutout in one of Guzmán's call centers, the account became the coalition's Rosetta Stone.

Taking the lead, Healy and his partners in Nogales started ripping Ofis-5 apart. Following a trail of BlackBerry chats, they moved from Ofis-5 to each of the ten or so lower-level accounts that it was sending orders to. The team in Arizona quickly realized that many of these junior accounts were getting orders from more than one Ofis account; instructions might be sent to them by Ofis-1 or Ofis-3 as well. Every time a new Ofis filter was discovered, Hogan got the corresponding phone number from Donovan. When he had his telecom informants ping the locations, all of the Ofis devices tracked back to Durango.[23]

As they slowly mapped the network, the coalition was starting to see the outlines of a pyramid. At the bottom of the pyramid, Guzmán's

---

23. Hogan has never revealed who his informants were beyond saying that some had legitimate access to the Mexican phone system and that others were drug traffickers, cooperating with the government, who had more clandestine means of hacking into it. It is possible that among his legitimate sources was Victor Vazquez's man in Guadalajara. Others may have worked for the Mexican military.

ground-level operatives—men like Speedy, Diablo and Memin—were checking in from cities around the world with the Ofis devices in Durango. Their message traffic was as heavy as ever: there were constant reports on drug loads moving from the jungles of Colombia or up the coast of California toward Seattle and Vancouver. The traffic in the opposite direction was equally busy: the Ofis filters were directing workers in the field to use certain airstrips or to hurry up and send their profits back to *El Gerente*. Every few days, however, the messages flowing through some of the accounts would drift into silence and sections of the pyramid would suddenly go dark. This, it was surmised, was a security precaution: the kingpin's men were changing their BlackBerry PINs or tossing their devices. During these blackouts the coalition scrambled. Scouring the wiretaps, they looked for clues and connections in the intercepts that could help them identify and track the new devices.

Sitting in Virginia, Donovan became consumed by the question of where Guzmán stood in this pyramid of mirrors. It was clear that the Ofis accounts were sending orders from the call centers to workers in the field. But who was sending orders to the call centers?

The coalition needed a different method of analysis. Through their wiretap approvals, each of the wire rooms not only had access to the heavy flow of BBM chats coursing through the system; they also had access to the metadata—or the toll records—for the BlackBerries they were tracking. Toll records are call logs: they document every device that any one particular device has been in contact with—and how often the contact has occurred. By crunching the toll records, Donovan assumed, the wiretap machine should be able to determine which devices on the network the Ofis accounts were getting most of their messages from. Ordinary people, using ordinary phones, get most of their messages from a parent, a spouse, a best friend. Drug traffickers, using pyramidal BlackBerries, get most of their messages from the boss.

By mid-July the toll record data had been analyzed. The Ofis accounts were getting most of their messages from two new devices with even more unusual screen names, which seemed to have been borrowed from two of Mexico's largest telecom providers: Telcel and Usacel. As soon as these devices were identified, Donovan sent their phone numbers to Hogan down in Mexico. Everyone was hoping that this "Second Tier" of the pyramid, as they were now calling it, would be Guzmán's tier. But when Hogan got the coordinates for Telcel and Usacel, they too came back as being in Durango. It didn't seem possible, but the new accounts appeared to be more cutouts in yet another call center. There wasn't just a single layer separating Guzmán from his workers in the field. There were two.

As deflating as the discovery was, Second Tier ultimately turned into a gold mine. The Nogales wire readers went to work at once, digging into Telcel and Usacel even more ferociously than they dug into Ofis-5. In short order, they unearthed several new Ofis accounts feeding into Second Tier and scores of new field accounts feeding into the new Ofis accounts. Second Tier, they determined, was a clearinghouse of sorts for everything beneath it, and pulling at its threads was like pulling at a weed in your garden and coming up with a huge root system with tentacles going everywhere. Soon Nogales and its sister wires were sucking up BlackBerry chats from every nook and cranny of Guzmán's organization. Through Second Tier, there were lines into his children, his girlfriends, his bodyguards, his plaza bosses, even his cooks and maids.

"At that point we realized what we had," Donovan said. "We'd broken Chapo's communications network. We had Speedy and Omega in Guatemala. There was great intel from the HSI wire from Central America to Canada. It was crossing with San Diego and crossing with New York. We were in a really good place."

Their mind-set, he said, wasn't just: *Let's keep going.*

Now it was: *Holy crap, we can actually capture these guys.*

SEVEN

Duck Dynasty

August 2013–January 2014

By high summer, things had reached the point where the coalition needed to meet, everyone in the same room, at the same time, face-to-face. Donovan and Hogan picked a date and place: August 21 at the embassy in Mexico. Invitations were sent out to New York, Chicago, Nogales, San Diego and several other DEA offices that had been pitching in from the peripheries: Phoenix, Miami, Long Island, Ecuador, Costa Rica and Vancouver. More than a hundred people were asked to attend, among them a few friendly members of the intelligence community. For the first time, Mexican counterparts, like SEMAR—the Marines—and the attorney general's office were brought into the fold.

In the run-up to the gathering Hogan sent Donovan an email proposing that each of the key participants do a PowerPoint presentation focused on how they planned to leverage what they had into takedowns of Guzmán, Mayo Zambada and other high-value Sinaloa targets. After the briefings, they would all split up to discuss their plans in smaller, separate breakout groups. Everyone agreed that the meeting should be geared toward real-world operations on the ground. In his note to Donovan, Hogan mentioned that next month, in September, some of their top subjects would probably be flying to Las Vegas for the big prizefight between Floyd Mayweather and the Mexican boxer Canelo Alvarez. Hogan suggested stopping those who went to Vegas at the airport and giving them a gentle exploratory squeeze for information.

Conspicuously missing when everyone sat down for the event in the embassy's crowded auditorium were Steve Marston and Bob Potash, the last two American agents to have gotten close to Guzmán. In advance of the meeting, Donovan had reached out to Marston in New York, extending an invitation. But he had received a curious response.

"He was very friendly," Donovan recalled. "He said, 'Give me a couple of days and I'll get back to you.'"

When Marston called back, he politely declined to join the coalition.

He and Potash, he explained, were doing their own thing.

That thing was Andrea Velez.

Exactly a year ago, after Christian Rodriguez had fled to the United States, the FBI's Operation Server Jack had found itself on life support. By late in the summer of 2012, Marston and Potash had missed their shots at Guzmán in both Cabo and Tepic, and had lost their access not only to the kingpin's encrypted cell phones but also to his FlexiSPY chats. Having lost their young informant too, the agents were facing a dispiriting situation: if they didn't find a new way of spying on their target, they might have to shut their mission down.

Both men were intrigued when their Spanish translator mentioned Andrea. Throughout 2012, Andrea had been showing up in Server Jack's one remaining endeavor: the iPhone intercepts that Marston and Potash were still collecting from Alex Cifuentes. Recently, the translator had noticed that Andrea's texts to Alex and her friends betrayed a certain level of anxiety. In her vulnerable state, the translator suggested, she might be a candidate for recruitment.

That September, Marston and Potash approached Andrea at the Bogotá airport, much like they had Rodriguez. Their timing turned out to be perfect. Andrea was by then in the advanced stages of a nervous breakdown triggered by the multiple murders that Guzmán and Alex were committing. Her own role in the plot to kill Rodriguez had pushed her over the edge. Only days before, she had dropped down onto her knees and prayed to the angels to rescue her. When the two FBI agents pulled her aside at El Dorado International, she decided they must have been the angels she was looking for.[24]

From Donovan's point of view, the embassy get-together was a huge success even without the FBI. His one thing—and he said it in the room—was that everyone on the team needed to be fired up, all in. After the gathering in Mexico, they were.

Within days of the meeting, the coalition was back at work in their scattered home-base offices. In San Diego, the Narco Polo wire room was pushing ever deeper into Mayo Zambada's world and was follow-

---

24. By the time Ray Donovan invited Marston and Potash to join the coalition, Andrea had been working undercover spying on Guzmán and Alex for nearly a year. But it took the FBI several months—until about mid-2013—to alert the DEA that one of its informants had infiltrated the kingpin's inner circle. Andrea had collected good information on Guzmán and Alex. In nightly phone debriefings with her handlers, she talked about the two men's operations in Canada and Ecuador, and mentioned visiting one of Guzmán's safe houses in Culiacán. Andrea also described the kingpin's movie project, inspiring a brief plot to lure Guzmán out of hiding by telling him that Hollywood was interested in his script. Though the plot was abandoned when Guzmán, for unrelated reasons, tried to kill Andrea, she did at one point to travel to Los Angeles to enlist the assistance of talent agents and producers.

ing a separate trail with their colleagues in Chicago that seemed to be leading toward Guzmán's chief of staff Damaso López and his son. Drew Hogan, sometimes at his desk until after midnight, was poring over messages from the pyramid's Second Tier, looking for the right piece of intelligence to turn the surveillance mission into a capture operation. Building out their own team in Nogales, Healy and his partners hired new translators and line sheet readers—they needed the extra help. As summer drew to an end, the Arizona wire room was exploding: hundreds of thousands of intercepts had already been collected and thousands more were streaming in each day from scores of BlackBerries all across the network. With the increased capacity, the overworked border mucks cast a wider net, moving past their initial targets, Speedy and Omega, to an ever-expanding circle that now included Guzmán's son, Iván Archivaldo; his father-in-law, Inés Coronel; and Cholo Ivan, one of his top killers. New figures also kept appearing. One of the latest was an errand boy of sorts who was often sent by the Office to take Guzmán's cars to the shop, fetch his meals and arrange his visits with prostitutes. His screen name was particularly memorable: El Nariz, the Nose.

In mid-September, Nogales homed in on another new figure: screen name Panchito. Panchito, by all of the evidence in front of them, was a major player in Guzmán's operation. According to the intercepts, he was overseeing much of the kingpin's business in Canada and had become involved in Ecuador with a ground-level worker named Rincon who was buying bulk shipments of cocaine from guerrillas in Colombia and moving them in airtight glass containers up to Mexico. When Donovan got the readouts on Panchito, he immediately suspected it was Alex Cifuentes—exciting news given Alex's close relationship with Guzmán. But there was less exciting news when Nogales, following procedure, ran Panchito's BlackBerry PIN through the federal government's deconfliction database. The search showed hits for the last American agents who had spied on Alex—and who might be spying on him now: the coalition's old friends, Marston and Potash in New York.

It was not the first time that the DEA and the New York FBI had crossed paths in the field while pursuing the same targets. This time, however, with the safety of the wiretap machine on the line, Donovan wanted to avoid a damaging collision. When the FBI called a meeting to discuss Cifuentes a few days later—at CIA headquarters in Langley, Virginia—Donovan showed up and came to an arrangement with the bureau and the agency. Everyone agreed that Alex Cifuentes should be arrested now that Nogales had tracked down his location. But there were differences of opinion as to who should make the arrest—and how and when it should occur. The DEA traditionally worked with the Mexican police; the FBI and the CIA with the army. Before the meeting ended, both sides reached a bottom line: Whoever took Alex into custody, it should be done in a way that did not disrupt anyone's ongoing investigations.

The deal did not exactly go as planned. Six weeks later the Mexican military launched a shotgun raid on the ranch outside of Culiacán where Alex was holed up with a crew of bodyguards from Guzmán's hit team, Los Antrax. The coalition had not been warned about the mission in advance and only learned about the furious gunfight that it triggered after the fact. Soon enough, the wiretap machine was picking up emergency alerts from Second Tier reporting on the battle and ordering the Ofis accounts to dump their devices simultaneously.

In virtually no time, big chunks of the pyramid went dark.[25]

* * *

25. Donovan declined to talk about the meeting in Langley. But Drew Hogan blames the FBI for tipping off the CIA about Alex's location and the CIA for subsequently tipping off the Mexican troops. Hogan seems to believe that the noisy raid on Alex was merely a case of bad management. In his book, *Hunting El Chapo*, he writes: "The CIA ... turned around and washed their hands of the whole ordeal after passing the

The arrest of Alex Cifuentes—in mid-November 2013—did more than just remove him from the table as a possible conduit to Guzmán. The temporary blackout it caused to the kingpin's communications system also threw a wrench into the coalition's most important project at the time: pushing past Second Tier to whatever was above it.

Hogan and Healy had been scratching at the problem since the meeting at the embassy and had in the meantime made a few discoveries. They had determined, fairly quickly, that Second Tier's accounts—Telcel and Usacel—were not being used by two different people but were almost certainly replica devices that the same person was using. They had also figured out, through toll record analysis, that Second Tier wasn't just talking with the Ofis accounts below it; it was also talking with a new account, one that seemed to be using helicopter models, like MD-8 and Bell-47, as its screen names. Intriguingly, whenever Second Tier chatted with this helicopter guy, he showed up in the intercepts as "Condor."

The breakthrough came when Nogales started digging into Condor toward the end of the fall. Condor's toll records were fascinating: they were different from those of any other device on Guzmán's BlackBerry network. The Ofis phones, for instance, communicated with both ground-level phones and Second Tier phones. Second Tier, meanwhile, communicated with the Ofis phones and with Condor's phone. But Condor, it seemed, communicated solely with Second Tier. His messages, that is, went in only one direction: down, not up. The pyramid of mirrors appeared to stop with him.

---

lead [to the army]—there was no oversight of the operation, and no close coordination with their Mexican counterparts." Others, however, have a darker interpretation. One person who worked with Donovan suggested that the CIA itself had been tracking Alex Cifuentes for months and had developed a proprietary interest in him. When Donovan and the coalition homed in on Alex, the agency encouraged the raid precisely so the DEA could not get the glory of arresting him. "It's all about dysfunction—and taking credit," this person said.

The coalition started calling Condor "Top Tier." They theorized that Condor was Guzmán's body man: the one standing next to him, receiving his instructions and passing them down along the Ofis system's complicated chain. Eager to locate Condor, Hogan rushed his Black-Berry PIN to Donovan and Donovan got the phone number that same day. When they pinged the number, Condor's coordinates did not track back to Durango like the Ofis devices or the Second Tier accounts. Condor's coordinates tracked back to Colonia Libertad, a ramshackle neighborhood in the heart of Culiacán, Guzmán's longtime lair.

By late November, with Top Tier now in sight, things began to suddenly speed up. While Condor had become the central target, the coalition didn't lack for others. Since the discovery of Second Tier that summer, Nogales and the other wires had been capturing BlackBerry chats from dozens, if not hundreds, of cartel operatives from Montreal to Guatemala City. Sometimes the intercepts were too good to ignore and the coalition would arrange for local authorities to swoop in on a subject and arrest him. Other times, it was better to be cautious and simply continue listening. It was always hard to make these decisions, which balanced action against gathering intelligence, especially since the coalition had no formal quarterback or shot caller. Ray Donovan could rightly describe himself as a coordinator, but he was in no position to unilaterally issue takedown orders, in foreign countries, on targets who might be under indictment in different judicial districts. To avoid more disasters like the one in Cabo—or the one involving Alex Cifuentes—the coalition developed a rule of thumb: If a high-value target stumbled into a situation where he might be grabbed easily, then, and only then, would they actually go grab him.

An early opportunity came on November 20, 2013, when one of Mayo Zambada's sons, Serafin, crossed the border not far from Jake Healy's office in Nogales to go Christmas shopping with his wife. As soon as Serafin set foot on American soil, he was detained on secret charges already on file in San Diego with evidence collected by the Narco Polo wire. A few weeks later, acting on a tip from the wire in New York, the Mexican police raided a beach resort in Puerto Peñasco, on the Gulf of California, and killed one of Mayo's top assassins in a gunfight while he was on vacation. The assassin, "Macho Prieto," had made the mistake of distancing himself from his power base in Culiacán, and the coalition, watching, had decided he was vulnerable. Then, on December 30, José Rodrigo Arechiga—or Chino Antrax, the leader of the Los Antrax hit team—left Mexico City for his own vacation in the extradition-friendly nation of Holland. The wiretap machine knew that he was going, and the Dutch police arrested him at Schiphol Airport in Amsterdam.

That same month, the coalition discovered another, much bigger, opportunity. Throughout the Christmas season, the wire room in Nogales had been picking up whispers that Guzmán was acquiring an unusual new collection of recreational equipment. There were suggestions on the wire that his men had bought him mud boots, hunting rifles, even a speedboat with a special airfoiled motor designed to drive on marshes. There were also indications that his four adult sons were regularly traveling from Culiacán to meet him at a mysterious vacation spot that they were calling "Pichis." While it wasn't quite clear where Pichis was, it seemed that Guzmán was setting up a kind of winter playground there. He had brought in a contractor to build him a swimming pool at Pichis and surrounded it with a few large palapas for afternoon barbecues.

Working with Donovan at SOD, Hogan and the team in Arizona began to track the kingpin's sons, pinging their locations over several days. From the GPS coordinates, they were able to determine that Pichis was somewhere in the sunny wetlands near the Ensenada de Pabellones, a small coastal waterway that fed into the Sea of Cortez, just south of Culiacán. Jake Healy, in his spare time, started doing research on the area. He discovered that the wetlands ecosystem was a migratory flyway, especially for ducks. One night, logging on to Google Earth, Healy took off from his desk in Nogales and sailed above the swamp in Sinaloa, cruising back and forth across the landscape until he found what he was looking for: a few dark smudges that seemed to be palapas. Moving in closer, he saw with a shock that the palapas were down the road from a well-known local tourist trap: the Pichiguila duck-hunting club.

No one could believe it, but it was right there on the map. The club at Pichis was a posh affair: an eco-chic resort with a dining gazebo and air-conditioned bungalows where hunters cooled down after mornings on the lagoon shooting at the rafts of pintails and gadwalls flying overhead. Guzmán's palapas were a few miles south of the club in a more remote stretch of the marshes. There was no one around for miles and the flat terrain, free of obstacles or hiding spots, was nearly ideal for an aerial assault. The coalition could not have invented a better place to stage a raid. They all started calling it Duck Dynasty.

"It was perfect for us," Donovan said. "It was out of the way and far from his usual stronghold. And he was going there pretty regularly."

Chasing Condor would have to wait; Duck Dynasty had now become the target. The next time Guzmán went there, the coalition would be going too—to grab him.

But first they had to find a partner. Which was always the catch in Mexico.

For many years, the DEA had worked with a special team of federal police called the Sensitive Investigative Unit, or the SIU, whose officers were trained and vetted by the agency itself. After the bungled raids in Cabo and Tepic, which were led on the ground—and perhaps also compromised—by the SIU, many of Donovan's law enforcement colleagues began having doubts about the unit and about the loyalties of the larger federal police force. Some of those doubts had been raised with Donovan when he sat down in Langley with the FBI and the CIA just before the army raid on Alex Cifuentes. The FBI was especially concerned about the federal police; in mid-2013, it had quietly assigned one of its top drug agents to investigate corruption in the force. By the end of that year, the agent's work confirmed to him what many in the US government already suspected: that the SIU and the federal police could, to a significant extent, be described as the uniformed enforcement wing of Guzmán's organization.[26]

As the raid on Duck Dynasty drew nearer, many of these critics undertook a pressure campaign to persuade the DEA to stay away from the federal police this time: the stakes were too high and the cops in Mexico were far too unreliable. The FBI and the CIA were once again pushing to use the army, but the DEA didn't trust the army any more than the bureau and the agency trusted the police. Others, among them the US Marshals, were advocating for the Mexican Marines. The Marines, they said, had the total package: they were driven, skilled and absolutely fearless.

Trained by the US military, the Marines had been used for years as an elite war-fighting unit and had only recently been called upon to serve on the home-front battlefield of fighting the country's drug cartels. Their first major anticartel mission was the bloody raid against Guzmán's enemy, Arturo Beltran-Leyva, in December 2009. It was typical of the Marines' esprit de corps that after they had killed Arturo, they covered his naked body in cash and put pictures of it on

---

26. The FBI's doubts about the SIU were borne out a few years later when Ivan Reyes Arzate, the unit's number-two man at the time of the Cabo raids, was indicted in Chicago. Reyes was accused of having been on the payroll of the Beltran-Leyva organization since at least 2007, just before it split from Guzmán's part of the Sinaloa federation. Even worse, in December 2019, Genaro García Luna, the man who once oversaw the entire Mexican federal police force, was indicted in Brooklyn on charges of taking millions of dollars in bribes from the cartel. García Luna pleaded not guilty to the charges shortly after they were filed.

the Internet. There were great personal dangers in treating traffickers like that: not long after the photographs appeared, some of Arturo's gunmen crashed the funeral of a Marine who had died in the raid and slaughtered several members of his family. There were also grave political risks. Guzmán had long been protected by the highest levels of the Mexican government. Staging an assault on him could easily put the Marines into conflict with their own civilian leaders. And yet when the coalition offered them the job, they took it.

"We asked them to go after Sinaloa and they did," Donovan said. "They took the challenge. In the eyes of the DEA and almost anyone else who had anything to do with this, they were national heroes. There should be monuments to them somewhere."

As the Marines began to plan their operation, so did the coalition. Many of the American faces were familiar. Jake Healy flew from Nogales to join Drew Hogan at the embassy and monitor the mission from a Mexican perspective. Donovan and his team at SOD holed up in Chantilly with their jigsaw-puzzle map, waiting for the moment when Guzmán headed south to Pichiguila. As soon as that happened, they planned to serve as a communications relay station, sending fresh leads, more or less in real time, from the wiretap machine to the operatives embedded with the Marines.

Donovan's link to the Mexican troops was another familiar face: Victor Vazquez, who had helped to oversee the raids in Cabo. Vazquez joined the new Marine strike force late in January when it set out from Mexico City and went down to its staging area at a naval base in La Paz, across the Sea of Cortez from Duck Dynasty. Vazquez's job was to eat, sleep and move with the Marines. He trained with the unit, rappelled with them out of Black Hawks, helped them analyze the feeds from the drones above the target zone and shared the accumulated wisdom of the wiretap machine to build what he was calling "a capture book" of intelligence. Vazquez, in a sense, was also in charge of operational security. The raid at Pichiguila had been kept under an exceedingly tight lid; but as the FBI's corruption investigator had recently discovered, the federal police were already trying to ferret out the details. Even the Marine commander at the base in La Paz was never told what his colleagues who had come down from the capital were up to.

Spirits were running high as the Marines moved into place on January 19. Hogan, sitting at the embassy, figured it would be a no-brainer. The helicopters would fly across the water, land at Pichiguila and nab the kingpin in his apron as he was grilling *carne asada*. The team in Nogales was also optimistic. ("We thought, hey, from an operational standpoint this could actually work," said their supervising agent, Matt Allen.) Donovan was particularly pumped. As the operation was about to launch, the wiretap machine had turned Guzmán inside out. It knew what he ate for dinner, where he went to parties and when he sent flowers to his girlfriends. "We had a sense of this man and this organization," Donovan said, "probably more than at any other time in history."

Just a few days earlier, the wire in Nogales had overheard the kingpin violating his own operational security. In a rare lapse of protocol, Guzmán had picked up a BlackBerry himself and traded several personal texts with his ex-wife Griselda López. Griselda, it appeared, had recently dropped by one of his safe houses in Culiacán and accidentally run into his latest mistress. Nogales caught her giving it to Guzmán in a cobra-necking string of BBMs.

2:35 P.M.: I know about your new acquisition, congratulations! Just remember that we stop loving but we always know how to appreciate! And you definitely abandoned us! That's why you don't do well in life, because in the end you are alone.

2:38 P.M.: Changing the subject. Please send me money for the month! . . . You owe me December and January.

There was only one note of caution being struck, and it was coming from another old hand who had joined the coalition: Brian Maxwell from the Marshals Service.

As a signals expert, Maxwell felt that the operational plan to take Duck Dynasty was flawed. He knew better than most that Guzmán and his men were no mere corner boys trading messages on pay phones and pagers. As impressive as the coalition's surveillance effort was, Guzmán's methods of countering it were even more impressive. The means and equipment he had at his disposal rivaled anything being used by the world's most sophisticated terror organizations.

Maxwell's primary concern was that the kingpin's network of spies and his closetful of snooping devices would detect the Marines before they put their boots on the ground, no matter how tightly the lid on the mission had been kept. If, or rather when, the operation was discovered, he imagined, the odds of Guzmán leaving Culiacán and going to Duck Dynasty were somewhere between nil and not a chance.

Maxwell was right.

On January 20, one day after Vazquez and the strike force of Marines arrived at the navy base in La Paz, the wiretap machine began to see disturbing messages on Damaso López's account:

10:04 A.M.: Good morning. Greetings to the COMPADRE and to you guys. Let COMPADRE know that the ones from the water are looking for an area to install themselves by the CONCHAL; rumor is that for a minimum of six months.

6:05 P.M.: Three "fast ones from the water" arrived at CASTILLO, all hooded ones (they're Special Forces from the water). Like they want to have an operation at El 19. The Commander is going to let us know later on once he talks to them. Let's see what he finds out.

6:21 P.M.: They're reporting four PFP trillas in LA CALMA. We have to be on alert in case they want to cross EL CHARCO.

9:14 P.M.: The guys from the water are investigating where the bridges are, seems they want to set up around there. The bridges of the PICHIGUILA by water are very close sir. And they are like twelve fast ones, four trucks, and one dually truck.

Special Forces from the water . . . An operation . . . We have to be on alert . . . Pichiguila . . .

The mission at Duck Dynasty was blown before it began.

EIGHT

The Baseball Field

Late one Sunday, in February 2014, Lucero Sánchez was at home alone in the house in Culiacán where she had been installed by Chapo Guzmán when she received a message that the kingpin wanted to see her. That's often how it was when you were the mistress of an international drug lord. Mistresses were expected to accommodate themselves to Guzmán's busy schedule. He wanted them to be on call around the clock awaiting orders, like any other member of the staff.

Small and dark-haired like most of the women in her lover's life, Lucero obeyed the summons. Leaving her house in Guadalupe, she made her way to another house in another neighborhood: Colonia Libertad, which lay closer to the banks of the brown Humaya River. When Lucero arrived in Libertad, she found the kingpin waiting at his table and joined him for a private meal, served to them as always by one of the maids who traveled with him everywhere he went. Their romantic evening didn't last long. Shortly after they sat down,

Guzmán's bodyguard rushed in and announced that the boss should leave. As Condor—Lucero knew him well—ran outside to start the car, Guzmán hurried up and collected his belongings. He told Lucero that he had to run some errands, but that once he was done he would send his man Nariz, the Nose, to get her. Then, without any further explanation, he was gone.

That, too, was often how it was: Guzmán had a habit of abruptly disappearing. In recent weeks, in fact, his distractions must have seemed especially intense. Lucero may have noticed that since the fall, the kingpin had been living in a kind of protracted panic. People around him kept getting arrested. First, it was his old friend Alex Cifuentes; then it was Serafin, Mayo Zambada's son. There had even been a close call with two of his own sons who were dining out in Culiacán one night when the military pulled into the restaurant's parking lot. With characteristic caution, Damaso López had begun to worry there were snitches in the organization—"fingers," he called them—whom he believed were secretly sending their BlackBerry PINs to the authorities. Damaso recommended changing the PINs more often and taking other measures like avoiding public meetings. The atmosphere of crisis had only gotten worse when reports arrived in January that a unit of Marines had moved into a naval base in La Paz. After that, there were daily—sometimes hourly—updates, keeping the boss informed about the placement of their helicopters and the movement of their troops.

Lucero was surely used to this by now. She had been dating Guzmán—if that was the word—for slightly more than three years. The two had been introduced at a party in the mountains in late 2010 and had quickly realized that they were both from Sinaloa and shared an upbringing rooted in the region's rural hardships. Lucero was from Cosalá, a farming village a few hundred miles from Guzmán's birthplace in La Tuna; like he himself, she had gone to work as a child. Her first job—at eight years old—was selling empanadas on the street; by ten, she was in her family's crop fields, tending to the corn and to-matoes with her parents. Though she later trained as a kindergarten teacher, she quit her career to marry a man from Tepehuanes, a poor part of Durango where the economy was based almost entirely on growing marijuana. Lucero's husband, a small-time dealer, beat her and she left him. At the time she was barely out of her teens.

When she met Guzmán a few years later, she was twenty-one and he was fifty-three. She must have been flattered when the world-famous drug lord showed her around the gathering in the mountains. In many respects, she was still a child at that point, working in a beauty salon and devoted to her family, while he was a wealthy celeb-rity with a global empire of thousands of employees. Everybody knew who Chapo Guzmán was, knew about the ballads that were written in his honor and knew that movie stars were after him to let them tell his story. Lucero even knew there was a bounty on his head—five million dollars, people whispered—but she didn't seem to mind.

After the party, the kingpin did what he would often do with women who caught his eye. One day, a man approached Lucero and handed her a BlackBerry. The device, he said, was from *El Señor* and had been specially "fixed" so that they could speak securely. When Guzmán called her—that same day or shortly after—he suggested that he wanted a relationship. What that turned out to mean was that the two of them saw each other once or twice a month. For a woman with Lucero's history, it must have been alluring nonetheless to have been thrust into a world of beachfront mansions and cloak-and-dagger secrecy, and their bond began to deepen—or at least it did from her side. By the end of that first year, she began to think of herself as the kingpin's partner or what she called his "home wife." She hemmed his pants, stocked his shelves with toiletries and went on little shopping trips to be certain that he always had new clothes.

Before long, there were other tasks as well. In late 2011, Guz-mán began to send her into the mountains on business missions to purchase marijuana. Meeting with local growers—men like her ex-husband—Lucero negotiated quantities and prices, and arranged to have his product shipped back to Culiacán below. It was dangerous work, requiring hours of navigating narrow roads and avoiding both the army and jealous rival dealers. But familiar with the people and the landscape, Lucero soon proved worthy. What she lacked in cunning, she usually made up for in devotion, stamping the kilos she acquired for her boyfriend with the logo of a heart.

She seemed to think that she was doing God's work, not just Guzmán's, bringing a steady income to the *campesinos* she had known her entire life. Perhaps that sustained her as she crossed the highlands for days on end, staying in her car so long she sometimes fell asleep behind the wheel. In spite of her exhaustion, she always found time to write the kingpin love notes in the evening, even if it meant she had to scramble up a hillside to be sure she got reception.

> **9:22 P.M.:** I want you to be proud of me, and I want you to know that from where I stand, in front of the Virgin, that I truly love you and miss you. . . . If there's a way for you and I to be together forever, I'll be the happiest woman in the world. . . .

After their demoralizing failure at Duck Dynasty, Donovan and his crew at SOD went back to work. For the better part of the next three weeks, as the ground team in Mexico waited for instructions and a fresh round of intelligence, they plugged into the wiretap machine from dawn until dusk until dawn again, sifting through its intercepts for any new leads or promising opportunities. "After January 20, it was basically nonstop," Donovan said. "We were going home to sleep for a couple of hours and coming right back." But even then, with the target still at large, no one really slept.

By early February, their grueling days and endless nights started to pay off. Guzmán was still avoiding Pichiguila, but the coalition had not lost sight of his bodyguard, Condor. From the moment that Nogales had identified Condor as the Top Tier of the pyramid, they had been tracking his movements, PIN-ing and pinging his coordinates through SOD with varying degrees of precision. Sometimes they had him in their sights; sometimes they did not. But all of the signals, when they managed to obtain them, came back to the same location: a single block, in a seedy section of Culiacán, called Colonia Libertad.

If Condor was indeed at Guzmán's side, then the block in Libertad could replace Duck Dynasty as the primary target. Again, however, it was not the only target. After Duck Dynasty, SOD had thrown the wiretap machine into overdrive: so much information was pouring in to so many different wire rooms from so many different BlackBerries that it now seemed possible to make a play for Mayo Zambada too. With the Marines impatient to strike—at something, anything—pressure was mounting to get what could be gotten and attempt assaults on both of the leaders simultaneously. The focused operation, which late in January had seemed on the edge of ruin, was suddenly expanded into a complicated, double-barreled mission. The coalition decided to go after Guzmán and Zambada at the same time, fixing on whichever one jumped first.[27]

Ultimately, Mayo jumped first. On the morning of February 13, the wire in New York picked up Mayo's "trigger" after spying on his maids. A lavish spread of Mexican food, the eavesdroppers determined, had just been ordered from the kitchens of his main estate at El Alamo, on the southern edge of Culiacán, and was on its way to a

---

27. As always, it was even more complicated than that. There was, in fact, a third target at the time: Miguel Félix Gallardo's old partner, Rafael Caro Quintero. Caro Quintero, often known as RCQ, had been released from prison that summer on a technicality after serving nearly thirty years for the 1985 murder of DEA agent Enrique Camarena. For many of Camarena's DEA colleagues, RCQ was the most important target of them all.

smaller ranch deeper in the countryside. The home-cooked meals—
enough to feed at least a dozen people—suggested that Zambada had
settled at the ranch with his security team. As soon as the intelligence
came in, Donovan and the agents in New York relayed it to Vazquez,
who quickly passed it on to the Marines. Late that afternoon, four
Marine Black Hawks with forty troops on board took off from the
navy base in La Paz and veered across the Sea of Cortez for the two-
hour flight to the target zone. Another fifty Marines had trundled
into pickup trucks and were closing in on Mayo to support the operation from the ground.

Despite the show of force—and the good intelligence—the raid
on Mayo was another failure. When the Marines descended on the
ranch, accompanied by Maxwell and Vazquez, all they found was a
caretaker, some baseball hats in a cupboard and an arsenal of automatic rifles buried in the yard. Donovan had to hand it to the wise
old man. After learning of the plans at Pichiguila, Mayo had packed
his bags and hurried off to his fortress in the country. The remote
location near El Alamo was no doubt guarded not only by his gunmen, but by sharp-eyed crews of lookouts, or *halcones*. It was all but
assured that as the strike team neared the property Mayo would be
tipped off in advance.

Guzmán had opted for a different path, taking refuge in his own
sort of fortress: his citadel in Culiacán. Having missed Zambada, the
coalition pivoted again and refocused its attention on the city. The
only question was: Who was going to go in there and get him?

No one relished the idea of walking into the lion's den. The Marines, who would be downrange, were especially apprehensive. The
best of the best, even they had never planned for a mission *inside* Culiacán, where Guzmán could go anywhere, at any time, with absolute
impunity. The coalition argued that its intercepts were solid. It was
true; they didn't have a street address for Guzmán yet. But the pings
on Condor's phone were tight and frequent and rarely strayed from

the block in Libertad. After the raid on Mayo, they admitted, some of Guzmán's Ofis-level filters had gone silent, but most of his BlackBerry network was still transmitting messages. There was one more thing that argued for a quick assault on Culiacán: the wiretap machine had recently been seeing hints that Guzmán was building tunnels in the city. One of the tunnels seemed to be connected to a safe house, in a web of similar houses, all of which were clumped in Colonia Libertad and the nearby neighborhood of Guadalupe, not far from the Culiacán baseball stadium. For now at least, the coalition was convinced that Guzmán was living in the area—the Baseball Field, they called it. But once his tunnels were built, it was impossible to know if that would last.[28]

After weighing their options and vetting the intelligence, the Marines decided they were in. Donovan, ecstatic, began to deploy the coalition's forces. Once again, he and his analysts at SOD would ride herd on the wiretap machine and remain on hand in Virginia to flip any PINs discovered in the raid into GPS coordinates. Hogan and Healy were headed up the coast to a military base on the Gulf of California where they would stay in touch with their colleagues in Nogales and feed the ground team the latest rounds of intercepts. At the tip of the spear, Vazquez and Maxwell would slip into the lion's den to conduct reconnaissance with a small group of Marines. Maxwell had the crucial job. Riding out front, in an unmarked car with some of the Marines, he planned to drive a grid through the Baseball Field, setting up his snooping gear to pinpoint Condor's phone. Trailing in a second car, Vazquez and more Marines would provide security, ensuring that as Maxwell found a door to hit, nobody got killed.

The ground team breached the city limits on the afternoon of February 16. Almost immediately, the kingpin's lookouts spotted

---

28. The coalition's intelligence about the tunnels had been confirmed by the FBI's informant Andrea Velez.

them. Phones started dropping up and down the pyramid as alerts went out through Guzmán's network that the Marines and the *gringos* were in Culiacán. Everyone assumed that Condor's phone would soon drop too, but Maxwell was having trouble finding it. The signal seemed to be coming and going as if Condor were moving in and out of range—or in and out of tunnels.

As darkness fell, the worst occurred: the police pulled them over. In a city like Culiacán, it was all but certain they would be on Guzmán's payroll.

The Marines weren't having it. Stepping from the trail car, one of their officers stood astride the threatening glare of headlights and, cradling his semiautomatic, advised the cops to go about their business. When the police drove off, Vazquez was impressed.

Their search, however, was over: Condor had caught wind of them by that point.

Bursting in on Guzmán's dinner with Lucero Sánchez, he had already rushed the boss from the house in Libertad.

Alone in Libertad, Lucero waited.

It was not unusual that Guzmán and his bodyguard had hurried off and left her on her own. But it must have seemed a little strange that after they had told her to stay put, the errand boy, Nariz, had still not come to pick her up. The young man, with his funny face and deferential manner, always obeyed the boss's orders. Biding her time a little longer, Lucero did the same.

Eventually she got new orders, but not from Nariz. One of the kingpin's maids called—that was strange as well—and told Lucero—strange again—to leave the house in Libertad and go to a different house, back in Guadalupe where her night had begun. When Lucero found the address, on Humaya Street, it was a house she'd never seen before, and she thought she had seen all of Guzmán's houses. This second house in Guadalupe was a modern beige two-story with two garage ports and a security camera posted at its door. It seemed ordinary in all respects but one: it sat behind a funeral home.

Guzmán was there to welcome her. In one of his expansive moods, he showed her the kitchen and the swimming pool outside, then led her in to the upstairs master bedroom.

Within an hour, he had fallen silent.

Lying next to him—alone again—Lucero couldn't sleep.

There was a reason why Nariz had not showed up that night. The Marines had already arrested him.

After they were stopped by the police in Libertad, Vazquez and Maxwell had given up on Condor. Condor, they decided, was much too slippery and Culiacán too hot. Dropping back to their command post, in a cornfield north of the city, they huddled in the darkness, running over options with the Marine commanders. If they could not find Condor, the man at Guzmán's side, there had to be someone else who knew where he was hiding. As midnight neared, it came to them: the errand boy, Nariz, the Nose.

Nogales went looking for intelligence. Scouring their wire, they saw Nariz had gone that night to a block party near one of Guzmán's houses in the Baseball Field. When Maxwell got them to the party—tracking Nariz's phone—the ground team found a few dozen people drinking under the stars on a noisy street, blocked by a pair of SUVs. The Marines moved in on the festivities, pulling aside the women and lining up the men in single file. As Vazquez walked down the row of anxious suspects, something caught his eye: another woman, off on her own, was hurrying toward a house across the street. Instinct told him: *Follow her.*

When the Marines burst into the house, they found Nariz hiding in the bedroom with his BlackBerry. A spot check showed its PIN was a match for the number that Nogales had been tracking. Vazquez had never met Nariz before, but the man in front of him just had to be the Nose: his nose was enormous, rising from his upper lip almost to the middle of his brow.

"Where's he at?" Vazquez barked. "I want to know where he's at right now."

"He's at the Three," Nariz blurted out—it was one of Guzmán's hideouts.

Vazquez knew he was lying. He already had the message from Nogales. Fresh off the wire, it had come in only minutes ago. Guzmán was at a different house—the Five.

When Vazquez confronted the Nose, he dropped his head and a long sigh cleared his chest of breath.

Sí, he admitted, looking up. The boss was at the Five.

Where Lucero Sánchez finally fell asleep.

When the news reached Donovan in Virginia, it was nearly three in the morning. By that point, he and his worn-out team at SOD had been working for more than twenty hours straight, but all hands hit the deck. They were electrified by the ground team's latest field report: Vazquez and Maxwell had tracked down the errand boy, Nariz. The next part was almost too good to be true: Nariz was going to help them find the Five.

The Nose had given them a block on Humaya Street—in the Guadalupe district, near the San Martín funeral home—but he either didn't know, or was too scared to provide, the exact address. He was claiming he would recognize the house when he saw it, and the coalition set about confirming his account. Nogales checked again on Condor's phone and it seemed to be back online: Maxwell was able to ping its new location off a cell tower in the neighborhood. The ground team had also found a cache of BlackBerry PINs in the call logs of Nariz's phone, and the analysts at SOD fed them to the wiretap machine, hoping to find corroborating intercepts or connections to Guzmán's other phones. Racing down to Culiacán from their base up the coast, Hogan and Healy sent out a group text with another little tidbit. They had both remembered that earlier in the day, the wire in Arizona had overheard Guzmán sending Nariz to the Five to meet his pool guy. It wasn't much, but it was something: the Five had a pool.

During all of this, Vazquez and Maxwell had been on the ground in Culiacán with the Marine commanders, sketching out the plans of an operation. It had come together quickly, in not much more than an hour's time, but Donovan approved. Given the kingpin's talent for escape, the Marines had quietly surrounded Humaya Street with a perimeter of troops and laid out a barricade of tire spikes on several nearby blocks. To maintain their edge of surprise, they were now proposing to approach the target block in two small, ordinary cars. The first car was Nariz's; in it was a clicker for the Five's garage door. Nariz himself, with one of the Marines at the wheel of the car, was prepared to lead the second car—with Vazquez and more Marines inside—slowly down the street and hit the clicker as they reached the right house. When the garage door opened, the rest of the strike force, lying in wait, would converge.

If the plan was not ideal, Donovan understood it was the best that could be hoped for, working on the fly, in the middle of the morning, with everyone exhausted. He didn't want to crowd his men, but could not resist checking in with them as they finalized the details. Was Condor's phone still pinging on the block in Guadalupe? Was Nariz still cooperative? Did the clicker still work? "I knew they had a job to do," he said. "But I remember thinking, This is it."

At four a.m., the signal came: mission imminent. In another few minutes, he would lose them.

The group chat buzzed with updates: *Perimeter secure. Strike force standing by. Cars now turning on Humaya Street.*

Just before his world went dark, Donovan got the final text.

The garage door was open. The men with battering rams were going in.

Lucero woke up to the pounding. The heavy thuds, in the calm of early morning, jolted her from bed. When she got up and went to the window, she might not have believed what she was seeing. Humaya Street was jammed with lights and vehicles. Helicopters hovered overhead.

Guzmán had barely stirred. But beside him on the nightstand, one of his security monitors showed a hive of grainy shapes slamming at the reinforced door in his garage. Looking closer, Lucero made out men in hoods and helmets.

Soldiers, she thought.

Forcing their way inside.

"Tío"—uncle—"open up! Tío, they're on us!" Condor was banging on the door.

Jolted up himself now, Guzmán ran to let him in, then hurried toward the bathroom. As Lucero ran after him, followed by the maid, there was another unreal sight: The kingpin, naked, was prying up one end of his bathtub.

Standing in the shower, he had popped the basin open like a car hood, exposing the giant hole that lay beneath it. In the hole, Lucero saw, was a wooden ladder descending through the floor.

"Come with me!" Guzmán shouted. "*Come!*"

She couldn't believe he wanted her to go in there. But he was already halfway down and, with little choice, she started down herself. The humidity hit her instantly, a damp heat laced with the stench of sewage. At the bottom of the ladder, she realized that they were in a tunnel.

Up ahead, Guzmán was cranking at the handle of a huge steel door that blocked their path, shouting out to Condor to hurry up and help him. When the two men forced it open, the three of them, with the maid in tow, raced into the sewers.

Lucero was traumatized. The air was rank, the ceilings low; there was barely any light. She could feel a pool of water covering her ankles and a coat of oozing sludge beneath her feet.

Rushing off, Guzmán and Condor left her with the maid. Soon they were out of sight.

Alone now, the two women stumbled through the darkness, following the filthy concrete walls.

Humaya Street had erupted into chaos.

Up and down the block, the Marines were running riot, ripping up manhole covers and stopping random strangers. Their radios blared. Their captains shouted orders. One of their hand grenades exploded in the Five.

Vazquez ran into the house with the second wave of the strike team and saw it when he reached the kingpin's bathroom: Guzmán's bathtub had been levered open at forty-five degrees on a set of hydraulic hinges; underneath it, a ladder led through a trapdoor in the floor.

Some of the Marines were down there now, pressing the chase and calling back that they could hear him. When Vazquez scrambled down to join them, they had already turned around. Ten feet forward, past a huge steel door, they were saying, it was *bajo, muy bajo*. They couldn't get much farther in. The tunnel was just too low.

Vazquez grabbed one of the captains. If the men went back, he said, without their long guns and their vests this time, maybe they could make it. The captain wasn't keen on the idea but once he thought it over, he asked for volunteers.

All of them volunteered.

At the mouth of the tunnel, Vazquez watched the Marines stripping off their body armor and strapping on their pistols.

"*Vaya con dios*"—go with God—he told each one as they headed back down.

Finally, the exit. Lucero could see it now, relieved.

It was a large stone drainage gate where the sewer spilled into the river.

Guzmán and Condor were waiting there for her and the maid. One by one they stepped into the water, wading through the shallows toward a small embankment then clambering up through the bushes to the street. Condor, on his phone, was already making calls to get them out of there. When he reached his friend Picudo, Guzmán's chief enforcer in the city, he ordered him to come at once and gave him their location. They seemed to be somewhere near the Federalismo Bridge.

Back on land the kingpin was panicked. He had been naked since he fled the house in Guadalupe and now gave orders for everyone to strip, right there on the riverbank, and give him their dry clothes. There wasn't time to wait for Picudo, he was saying. The troops were on their tail. They had to steal a car.

But there wasn't one to steal. They were on a small road, in the darkness, at four in the morning, with nothing much around except a few locked houses and the National Water Office.

Picudo was the best chance they had, perhaps their only chance.

And he was already on his way.

An hour after the strike team discovered Guzmán's tunnel, the men in the field finally came to life. Maxwell started to answer Donovan's group chats, if single words were actually an answer. In the heat of the chase, there wasn't much he could report.

What do you got? . . . Nothing.

You have him yet? . . . Negative.

"You talk about pins and needles," Donovan said. "For a drug agent—for anyone—this is the highest point you'll reach in your career."

The lowest point arrived at seven in the morning in Virginia when Donovan got the text he had been hoping to avoid.

We missed him. He's in the wind.

Everyone at SOD knew what was coming next. All of the Black-Berries they'd been tracking would be dumped. They were going to lose the wiretap machine.

It was Donovan's first real taste of Guzmán's cunning; he did not like it. It seemed the man knew everything that was going on around him. He knew that the Marines were coming. He knew where they were going. He even knew that his own men had been with them. That kind of savvy, Donovan thought, that kind of *awareness*, only came with protection at the highest levels.

The one good piece of news that morning was Nariz. After leading the ground team to the Five, Nariz had taken them on a dawn-light tour of Culiacán. Driving them through the Baseball Field, he showed them Guzmán's four other safe houses, each one connected by a similar bathtub tunnel. Moving on, he led them to warehouses, stash houses and several private houses, among them Condor's house and a large house filled with modern art that belonged to Guzmán's ex-wife Griselda.

When the tour was over, the kingpin's local infrastructure was in shambles. The Marines had seized thirty high-end vehicles and an arsenal of RPGs and automatic weapons. They had found Guzmán's own weapon, a pistol with his initials monogrammed in diamonds on the handle. They had even found a crate of plastic bananas, each one loaded with a filling of cocaine.

Donovan had gotten reports about all of that too. But it didn't take the sting out.

He was still out there, waiting to be found.

If only somebody could find him.

Pulling up in a red sedan, at shortly after four a.m., Picudo, the enforcer, had found him by the river. As the boss piled into the car with Condor and the women, Picudo was told where they were going: Mazatlán, one of Guzmán's other stronghold cities farther down the coast.

At a high rate of speed, it is a two-hour drive from Culiacán to Mazatlán, the shortest route being Highway 15D. The sun, then, would have just been coming up when the fugitives were dropped at a beach resort north of the city center, a dawn-light tour of their own.

It was one of Donovan's analysts who noticed it. As the day ground on in Chantilly, he realized that the man they knew as Picudo had been moving.

San Diego had been tracking Picudo since the summer and everyone was a bit surprised that even after the close call at the Five, he hadn't dropped his BlackBerry. According to Picudo's pings that morning, he had been in Culiacán at four a.m. Then he was in Mazatlán at six.

What caught the analyst's eye was what happened after that. The pings made it fairly clear that after going down to Mazatlán, Picudo had turned around and come straight back.

SOD was trying to figure it out. Picudo was one of Guzmán's most trusted soldiers, his chief enforcer and plaza boss in Culiacán. Why, they wondered, had he gone to Mazatlán at all? And why had his trip been so abrupt?

Only one reason: he had taken Guzmán to Mazatlán.

Donovan was on the phone at once with Brian Maxwell.

"Brian," he begged, "you have to drop to Mazatlán."

Maxwell, after hearing the news, agreed. "We'll lift and shift," he said.

Before they did, however, there was one more job to do in Culiacán. They had to pay a visit to Picudo.

Manuel López Osorio—better known as Picudo—was fast asleep at his modest ranch house on the western edge of Culiacán, not far from the airport. The past two days had been exhausting.

On Monday morning, the day before, Picudo had been woken at a little after four by his old friend Condor with panicked orders to fetch him and the boss near Segunda Street by the river. When he rushed to pick them up, he learned he was to hurry them—and the women they were with—to Mazatlán, a two-hour drive down the Sinaloa coast.

Stopping at a turnoff on the highway, Picudo had passed his charges, at shortly after dawn, to his counterpart in Mazatlán, "Bravo" Aponte, who oversaw the city for the kingpin. Then, with his mission finished, he received new orders: turn around and head back up to Culiacán.

Stranger things had happened to Picudo over the years. The one strange thing about that trip, he remembered, had been Guzmán himself, who had seemed a little out of sorts and sullener than usual.

Or so he said, at two on Tuesday morning, when a group of armed Marines, arriving with the *gringos*, broke through his door and arrested him in bed.

The arrest of Picudo and his subsequent confession—early on the morning of February 18—was the coalition's best evidence yet that after fleeing the Five, Guzmán had in fact left Culiacán and taken refuge in his second city, Mazatlán. It was not, however, their only evidence at that point. Even at that fragile phase of the search, the wiretap machine was seeing more activity than Donovan had expected. Hours earlier, San Diego had picked up hints that another one of Guzmán's gunmen—alias Popeye—was also in Mazatlán, perhaps to augment his security team. Separate intercepts suggested that infusions of cash, lots of cash, were on their way to Bravo Aponte, the kingpin's local plaza boss.

While Donovan had quite a bit that was pointing him toward Mazatlán, what he did not have yet was a target in the city, a busy port town with a crowded coastline, an international airport and more than four hundred thousand residents. His colleagues in Nogales were pinning their hopes on a powerful new tool for homing in on Condor, who still remained the best chance for homing in on Guzmán. For weeks now, the team in Arizona had been working with Andrea Goldbarg, a prosecutor in Washington, DC, to obtain what was called a roving wiretap on the kingpin's bodyguard. Roving wires permit investigators to follow specific subjects, not just their devices, meaning that no matter how often Condor changed his PIN or dumped his phone, Nogales would be able to stay with him. Though the team was getting close to its approval, the process was notoriously difficult and no federal judge had ever given permission for a roving wire on foreign soil. As Nogales waited eagerly to hear from chambers, Donovan and his own team had undertaken a different way of tracking down the kingpin. They had asked the wiretap machine, and the intelligence community, to spy on Guzmán's maids.

After almost a month of twenty-hour days—a marathon that had begun in January with the planning at Duck Dynasty—what they all really needed was a break. If they didn't take one, it was only because their target hadn't taken one and they felt that he was near the end of his rope.

"Sometimes it's better having someone try to run from you," Donovan said, "because that's when they expose themselves. When you run, you make mistakes."

It is unlikely that anyone paid much attention when the old man in the wheelchair was rolled into the Hotel Miramar in Mazatlán that Friday by a younger man who may have been his son. The pale pearl condominium tower, a twelve-story pile on the Avenue del Mar near the beach, was, with its discount rates, a haven for retirees and tourists. Rental leases in places like the Miramar tend to be relaxed affairs. They are often agreed upon informally, settled both quickly and in cash.

There was, of course, a register for the hotel's guests and tenants. But all it said on that day, February 21, was that the young man taking Apartment 401 was named *Allon*.

When the judge in Arizona formally approved the roving wire on Condor, Vazquez, Maxwell and Hogan were on their way to Mazat-lán with a small group of Marines.

It was February 21, a good day.

To confuse the *halcones*—the lookouts—all of them had stopped, before leaving Culiacán, at a Soriana discount store, where they traded in their uniforms for flip-flops and board shorts, as if they were sunseekers headed to the beach. Driving south, they split up on the highway, moving one car at a time. For extra security, they had commandeered vehicles that had been seized that week during the raids on Guzmán's armored fleet.

Word of the roving wire reached them on the road at more or less the same time it reached Donovan at SOD. Hogan immediately pinged Condor's number in one of Guzmán's cars. Donovan pinged it at his office in Virginia. Both came back with the same rough set of coordinates: the Hotel Miramar, a pale pearl condominium tower in Mazatlán, on the Avenue del Mar.

It wasn't much, Apartment 401. A kitchen, a sitting room, a little front-hall alcove and a pair of small bedrooms. But at the rate they were paying, Señor Allon and the old man in the wheelchair could make do.

It soon got crowded in the fourth-floor suite, however. Later that day, the old man's wife—or was it his daughter?—came to join him. She was not alone, having brought along her two baby girls, the nanny and a maid.

As he drove past the Miramar, after getting in to Mazatlán that evening, Brian Maxwell's snooping equipment registered a hit.

Condor's phone was in the building. The target was confirmed.

At work at SOD that night, Donovan was in his usual state of high anxiety. His own job was finished; now it was the ground team's job to bring Guzmán in.

As he had done with Culiacán just days before, he had talked with Vazquez and Maxwell about how they planned to hit the hotel's door.

Over the years, Donovan had made plenty of his own plans to hit plenty of his own doors. He knew that he was working with the best, but he also knew that well-laid plans—and well-placed doors—sometimes didn't work.

The ground team and the Marine commanders settled in at a large white house in a residential district of the city far from the noise and neon of the waterfront. For Mazatlán, it was quite the palace, with a Greek facade and a pleasant courtyard garden. After ordering pizzas, the excited men went to bed at ten. If the *halcones* found them here, they deserved to get a bonus.

The following morning, they set out in the dark of four a.m. From their makeshift base, it was two long turns to the Avenue del Mar.

When their trucks pulled up beneath the line of palm trees in front of the Hotel Miramar, Victor Vazquez—no doubt thinking of Cabo—immediately sent a few Marines around to the back. He posted others by the swimming pool and underneath the tall facade of balconies. His orders to them could not have been clearer: he wanted to be notified at once if anyone so much as poked their head out.

The only problem with the mission, as far as he could tell, was the size of the strike team the Marines had brought: twenty-four men, stretched thin past his liking.

Okay, he thought as the perimeter was set and he glanced up at the building. *He's got to be in there somewhere.*

Somewhere, yes. But where?

According to the guest register, two new groups of tenants had arrived the day before. One was a certain Señor Allon who was staying on the fourth floor with his family. The other was a pair of younger men with Anglo-sounding names who had taken a sixth-floor luxury apartment, overlooking the water.

Some on the ground team reasoned that the famous drug lord Chapo Guzmán would obviously take the room with views.

But then there was an alternate theory: Perhaps he was avoiding deluxe accommodations in favor of laying low.

Somewhere, yes. But where?

* * *

Luz verde—green light—in the hour before dawn.

Sitting in Virginia, his world gone dark again, Donovan couldn't help but wonder:

Was it possible to build a tunnel *under a hotel*?

Luxury won.

After crashing through the door of the sixth-floor ocean-view apartment, the strike team of Marines found two young stoners sleeping off a night of smoky revels. They were scared to death, of course, and at least at first not entirely coherent. But under the tonic of an armed interrogation, they were absolutely certain about one thing: they had nothing to do with Chapo Guzmán.

The ground team was unsure. There was weed in their room, and that was something. But one of the stoners was clearly an American. He even had a California medical marijuana card.

Had Guzmán started using trained American killers as his bodyguards?

Unsure.

On the fourth floor, meanwhile, Señor Allon was asleep in the front hall alcove near the door. In the smaller bedroom, on separate beds, were the two young girls, the nanny and the maid.

Down the hall, in the master suite, the old man slept beside the woman—his wheelchair, no longer needed, safely stowed in the sitting room.

In bed together.

So clearly not his daughter then—his wife.

*   *   *

Brian Maxwell, a proponent of the alternate theory, sat on the front steps of the Hotel Miramar, his back bent, head in hands. It was happening again. They were going to lose him. Again.

The main Marine strike team had tied itself in knots with a couple of harmless dopers while the world's most wanted criminal was two floors beneath them, perhaps cocking his rifle, if he was even still there. The street outside was flooded with activity by now, Mazatlán was rising, and no one seemed to be listening. Until Maxwell found a Marine lieutenant who finally called his captain.

When he ran him through the situation, the captain nodded, giving him a handful of men.

New target: Apartment 401.

In and up, they went.

They didn't need a battering ram this time. The door was that flimsy.

Marinas!

Condor had a weapon, but stepping from the alcove near the front door, he lowered it at once.

In the smaller bedroom: the maid, the nanny and the little girls, their matching pink suitcases lying on the floor.

Racing back toward the master bedroom, the Marines found Guzmán's wife, Emma Coronel, alone in bed. "Don't kill him!" she pleaded, looking toward the bathroom. "Please, don't kill him!"

Guzmán had dashed toward the toilet with a Bushmaster semiautomatic. His wife screamed not to shoot him. The Marines, their rifles leveled, told him to come out.

Okay, all right, *bueno*, he was coming out.

*   *   *

On Vazquez's radio, the confirmation signal: *Siete! Siete! Siete!*
They had him.
They had him?
He ran toward the hotel's underground garage.

In the custody of the Mexican Marines were:

Carlos Hoo Ramírez, also known as Condor; Emma Coronel Aispuro, Chapo Guzmán's wife; one of the kingpin's maids, alias Chaparra; and the nanny charged with caring for his two young daughters, Kiki and Emalia.

When Vazquez came around the corner, hurrying down the garage's spiral driveway, he saw Guzmán kneeling on the asphalt, shirtless and surrounded by Marines.

Holy shit, he thought, *it's really him.*

As Vazquez approached, someone took a photograph.

Standing over Guzmán, he whispered to his target, "*Eres tu.*"

It's you.

When news of the capture was blasted out on the coalition's group chat, Donovan—the words did not do justice—was elated. "We were just on top of the world," he said. "Basically like kids in a candy store."

Everyone was congratulating one another, getting a little giddy. *Hey man, couldn't have done it without you. . . .*

But it was true. There was no way the DEA could have done all this alone. Or HSI. Or the Mexicans. "None of us could have done it on our own," Donovan said. "But because it was all of us together, it validated all of our work."

The photograph, for instance.

Donovan had gotten it from Hogan and Maxwell on the ground and quickly passed it on to his team at SOD. From there, it went to the assistant chief and the chief of the division, then on to headquarters in Washington.

Flying over agency walls, it sailed toward Justice, Homeland Security, even the FBI, before making a left on Pennsylvania Avenue.

There, it finally landed, in the Oval Office of the White House, on the desk of the president himself.

INTERLUDE

Chivo Expiatorio

Shackled at the wrists and sandwiched between three Marines in ski masks, the world's most wanted man was on the move. Within hours of his arrest, Guzmán was placed on a military Learjet and flown to Mexico City. There he was presented at a perp walk for reporters in a pair of handcuffs and a crisp white dress shirt. It was not much after noon on a Saturday in February, but seizing on the weekend news, the global media was already in a frenzy. The Associated Press, having gotten the initial tip, was first in reporting that the "legendary outlaw" was in custody, noting that his "larger-than-life persona" and his place in "Mexican folklore" had been unable to assist him this time. To the *Telegraph*, Guzmán was a "mythical figure"; to *El País*, he was "the most important narco that has ever been." *The New York Times* paid homage, somewhat staidly, to the drug lord's "legend" and the "mystery of his whereabouts." It also obtained a quote from a source on the ground who shared his opinions on Guzmán's ambiguous ontology. "He was somebody who existed," this philosophical man-on-the-street explained, "and didn't exist."

In the welter of words and images that day, it wasn't the worst description. His own kind of centaur—half man, half make-believe—the kingpin had always occupied the hazy space that sat between reality and fairy tale. It was often impossible with Chapo Guzmán to know where the folklore ended and the facts began. The anecdotes about his life and crimes had been passed from hand to hand so often they had finally acquired the edgeless quality of fables. Was it really true, as the newspapers said, that during his early days in the mountains he would come down out of hiding for lavish meals in Culiacán and have his men collect the cell phones of all the other diners in the restaurant? And what about the story he told to Javier Rey about the time that soldiers took him into custody in Nayarit and flew him upside down, hanging him by his ankles, from a helicopter?

This sort of narrative broad-mindedness was familiar to many in Mexico and was especially well known in Sinaloa, riven as it was by a tradition of inequality and the sort of social hardships that inspire magical thinking. The particularities of history had prepared the state for Guzmán's outsize legend. For more than a hundred years, Sinaloa had been ruled by a caste of powerful *caciques*, local strongmen who nominally ran the region for the federal authorities, but were in practice more like feudal lords, accountable to little beyond their own ambitions and avarice. As the state industrialized in the middle nineteenth century, their plunders of the poor triggered the emergence of a class of outlaws who often conflated profitable brigandage with political rebellion. Much like Robin Hood had skirmished with and stolen from the landed gentry of Nottinghamshire, men like Heraclio Bernal (1855–1888) and Felipe Bachomo (1883–1916) robbed and revolted against the nobles of Sinaloa. Over time, these real-life radical bandits coalesced in the state's imagination into the single mythic figure of Jesus Malverde, the so-called narco-saint.

The legend of Malverde, though historically unverified, is revered in Sinaloa, where it has been handed down from fathers to sons since the moment of its creation. Born in 1870, Malverde was said to have been raised in the region when it was under the thumb of Governor Francisco Cañedo, who carried out a repressive policy of economic expansion for the ruthless dictator Porfirio Díaz. Malverde's parents were apparently so penniless they starved to death, leaving him to fend for himself in a job on the Mexican railroads where he was exploited by a string of brutal bosses. Looking for a better life, and perhaps vengeance, he moved to the mountains with a band of hardy men who joined him in his quest to rob from the rich and give to the poor. But Cañedo put a bounty on his head, and one of Malverde's men eventually betrayed him. After his capture, in 1909, Malverde was put to death, either shot by a firing squad or hanged by the police.

Eighty years later, when Chapo Guzmán started his career, generations of narco-traffickers had already co-opted Malverde's saga to justify their own business model of stealing, as they saw it, from the drug-addled *gringos* in the north and repatriating the profits back to Mexico. In this retelling of the story, the narcos—like the bandits of old—were heroes: a ragtag bunch of poor kids from the mountains who slipped across the border and returned with treasures for their families. There is some evidence that as Guzmán's fortunes grew, he too shared a portion of his wealth in Sinaloa (he was particularly fond of building churches). But the idea that he, or anyone around him, was engaged in a program of redistributing assets is a fable built upon a fable. Guzmán's real progenitors were not Malverde or Robin Hood; they were Houdini and the Road Runner.

For more than a decade before his arrest at the Hotel Miramar, Guzmán had been staging public spectacles, enacting evasions and escapes to the glee of many ordinary people who were saddled with a history of abuse and neglect by the authorities. If his magic tricks were not in fact magic, but engineered events, carefully oiled by government graft, it didn't matter. Or at least it didn't diminish the schadenfreude-like pleasures of watching him perform his act.

That was what was not getting through in the media frenzy following his capture: the kingpin's legend wasn't simply based on his enviable fortune or his startling longevity or his time-proven talent for slipping away; it was based on how all of these qualities conspired together to expose the fecklessness and corruption of the government. Every time that Guzmán managed to be there one minute, gone the next, it reinforced a preexisting belief that Mexico's rulers were the fools that everyone assumed them to be. Every dollar that Guzmán spent on bribing the authorities had a double purchasing power: it served not only to protect him and his interests, but to prove—as if more proof were needed—that the guardians of the country's body politic were unworthy of its trust. "Today I believe more in El Chapo Guzmán than I do in the governments that hide truths from me," Kate del Castillo had tweeted two years earlier. After the events in Mazatlán, a perceptive professor said something similar to a Mexican reporter: "With the state of things in Mexico, the situation is truly interesting. . . . The idols, the heroes, who should be official figures of moral integrity, decency and honor, don't exist."

That Guzmán had been arrested, despite this lack of official integrity, in no way contradicted the idea that on the whole the Mexican authorities were compromised. Nor did it contradict the idea that the American authorities who had helped in his arrest were hindered by their own moral failing—namely, a recurrent inability to get along with one another. The capture operation that began near Pichiguila, moved through Culiacán and ended on the Avenue del Mar was distinguished by its technical expertise and its sheer dogged persistence. But it was also blessed by no small amount of happy accident. With Guzmán, it had always been like that. "We understood pretty quickly that there was only one way to get him," said Thomas Shakeshaft, a Chicago prosecutor who pursued the kingpin for a decade. "It wasn't enough to just be good. You had to be a little lucky too."

And yet, for some suspicious souls, even hard work leavened by a bit of luck was not enough to account for the success of getting Guzmán off the streets. There had to be something else at play, and in the dark world of the drug war that usually meant a conspiracy. Even as Guzmán was sent to prison, the Mexican media was full of knowing whispers. The kingpin, it was said, had overplayed his hand and had finally lost the trust of his government protectors. Unless, of course, his partner, Mayo Zambada, tired of the heat that he had long brought down on the cartel, had decided to turn him in.

There is no shortage of conspiracy theories concerning Chapo Guzmán. Discussing the kingpin in an academic treatise on Mexican cartels, the sociologist Jim Creechan correctly notes that it was he—and not the equally guilty Mayo—who first became the face of the international drug trade.[29] To Creechan, Guzmán's prominence, reaching back to the early 1990s, presents a paradox—"the paradox of visibility"—because prominence runs counter to the normal way of mafia bosses, who tend to operate in quiet anonymity. This "narco-stardom," as Creechan calls it, suggests that Guzmán was actually much less powerful than Mayo, and that he may indeed have been elevated to his celebrated status in order to distract the world from the crimes of other colleagues.

Creechan's argument—and he is not alone in making it—goes like this: In 1993, after the assassination of Cardinal Ocampo, Mexico's then president, Carlos Salinas de Gortari, found himself in an untenable position. Salinas, on the one hand, needed for political reasons to get tough on organized crime and assuage the public outrage that the cardinal's killing had occasioned. On the other hand, Salinas could

---

29. Creechan's work comes from a draft chapter on Guzmán in a book currently titled "Cartels and Drug Violence."

not be too hard on the traffickers, given the central role they played in his economy and, worse, the information that they had on his own administration's involvement in the drug trade.

Caught between this rock and a hard place, Salinas supposedly opted for a third way: diverting the attention of his country onto a *chivo expiatorio*, or scapegoat. "El Chapo Guzmán became the sacrificial lamb," Creechan writes. "The government . . . moved to muster evidence that the Chapo Guzmán narrative represented the most credible explanation of the murder, and simultaneously and improbably, initiated a plan to persuade the world that this insignificant and uneducated man from Mexico's western Sierra Madre was the most important boss of Mexico's most important drug cartel." Following this "ritual elevation," everyone apparently went home happy. Salinas, appearing to do something by jailing Guzmán for Ocampo's death, reduced the pressure on his government to do too much. Guzmán's rivals in the drug trade—among them Mayo Zambada and the Tijuana drug cartel, which had actually killed the cardinal—were spared the pains of a crackdown. Even Guzmán seems to have gotten something in the bargain: "a payout or trade-off from other cartel leaders" for gradually agreeing to accept the blame.

As seductive as all of this may be, it suggests the lengths to which otherwise reasonable people will go in trying to explain the allure of Chapo Guzmán. A cottage industry has in fact sprung up with the sole goal of accounting for his myth. What often ends up happening is that one myth is substituted for another. If it seems unlikely that an insignificant, uneducated peasant from the western Sierras could rise to become the maximum boss of the Mexican drug trade, then surely the president of Mexico put him in the post; or his cunning partner maneuvered him into taking it; or Central Intelligence, fearing what he might reveal about its own operations in the country, secretly helped him out along the way.

Though perhaps less satisfying as an answer, it could simply be that

Guzmán's myth arose from the way in which his natural talents—for corruption and escape—played in front of a specific local audience, one that thrilled to see the government embarrassed. It is certainly the case that Guzmán was tenacious—and a little lucky—just like the law enforcement officers who tracked him down and captured him. The kingpin was, by all accounts, obsessed with his profession, a workaholic who never shut up about the office. "Chapo always talks about the drug business wherever he is," one of his first employees, Miguel Angel Martínez, once said. "With whatever people he's with, he's talking about drugs."

Guzmán also started his career at an auspicious moment: in the early eighties just as demand for cocaine was reaching its peak in the United States. At the end of the decade, he was further helped when, under pressure from American officials, the Mexican authorities arrested his mentor, Miguel Félix Gallardo, dismantling the old regime and creating space for fresh blood from below. As Guzmán found his place in the power structure after Félix Gallardo was imprisoned, NAFTA came along, deregulating the border and ravaging local agriculture. The sudden spike in international trade made it infinitely easier to ship drugs north, hidden in the endless streams of cargo trucks; it also persuaded many farmers to switch to illicit crops or to leave their land for crowded urban slums. There, devoid of options, some began to work for the cartels.

Driven by ambition in a booming market filled with opportunity, inventory and labor, it may not have taken a complicated conspiracy to have launched Guzmán into celebrity—especially when he himself relished being celebrated.

Just before the Marines swooped down on him in Mazatlán, he had put the finishing touches on the *El Padrino* movie project. Working with his assistant, Andrea Velez, he had lovingly assembled an eighteen-page promotional package for the film, complete with a biography section ("Who is Joaquín Guzmán Loera?") and a scene-by-scene synopsis of its episodes. The Mexican actor Gael García Bernal had been tentatively cast as the young Chapo Guzmán, with John Leguizamo slotted for the supporting role of Pablo Escobar. The "paradox of visibility" was paradoxical only in the sense that Guzmán never wanted to be invisible; he wanted to be seen.

Third Strike

Myth is neither a lie nor a confession:
it is an inflexion.

—Roland Barthes

NINE

A Hole in the Shower

The captured kingpin, now more notorious than ever, left Mexico City late in February to await his fate in the country's most forbidding federal prison, the Social Readaptation Center No. 1. Better known as Altiplano for sitting on a high plain forty miles from the capital, near the city of Toluca, Guzmán's new home was a multitowered fortress, bathed in spotlights and surrounded by razor wire and a vast expanse of crop fields. Not one of the major traffickers who had been jailed there over its twenty-three years had ever escaped. Altiplano's walls were built of concrete three feet thick; its cells and corridors were monitored by cameras; its local airspace, a no-fly zone, was heavily restricted. Jamming devices had been put in place to prevent the inmates from communicating with the outside world. Shortly after Guzmán was brought to the prison, the administration clamped a bracelet on his wrist armed with a GPS transmitter. CISEN, the national intelligence service, posted two employees to its operations center. Given the kingpin's previous escape, they were taking no chances. The spies watched Guzmán around the clock on a closed-circuit television set.

Even under these austere conditions, Guzmán started planning his escape from Altiplano within days of his arrival. To communicate with his conspirators, he worked through two accomplices, both with visitation rights. One of them, predictably, was his longtime lawyer, Oscar Gomez, a veteran of his many secret schemes and operations. The other, perhaps more surprisingly, was his young wife, Emma Coronel.

Though not yet twenty-five, Emma occupied a unique position in the hierarchy of hundreds that surrounded her husband. While she was not in any formal sense a member of the Company, as his organization sometimes called itself, she had long been complicit in a number of his crimes. In 2012, Emma had helped Guzmán evade his pursuers in Los Cabos and had often acted as a proxy in his phone calls with her father, Inés Coronel, who had worked with the boss for years running operations on the Arizona border. As the kingpin's wife, Emma enjoyed a privileged primacy in the world of the cartel and clung to it with an aptitude for power that was virtually the equal of his own. Though she may have looked like the former beauty queen she was, her strappy heels and plastic enhancements disguised a mind that was either void of moral sensitivity or was sufficiently conniving to project an air of innocence and ruthlessness at once. If Lucero Sánchez was the kingpin's tool and mistress, Emma was his partner. Her loyalty to Guzmán seemed unquestionable. But whether it was based on love, fear or material comfort was impossible to tell.[30]

---

30. According to the well-worn legend, Emma Coronel Aispuro, a small-town girl from La Angostura, Durango, first met Chapo Guzmán in 2006 after she was crowned the region's local Coffee and Guava Queen. Guzmán is said to have attended a dance party following the pageant, arriving with as many as two hundred gunmen riding ATVs. A year later, in July 2007, the couple was married. The wedding—Guzmán's third (or possibly fourth)—was a modest affair of accordion music and local politi-

Perhaps it didn't matter: within a month of her husband being sent to Altiplano she was already involved in the plot to set him free. The mission planning, at his direction, was divided into two parts. Oscar Gomez took charge of assembling a crew of outside experts: a financier to fund the venture; straw men to buy the real estate they needed; and an engineer who devised the means of the prisoner's escape. Emma's job was to enlist a separate circle of collaborators from among the kingpin's relatives and lieutenants. One of the first she spoke to was Damaso López, Guzmán's chief of staff.

Meeting with Damaso in Culiacán, in March 2014, Emma conveyed her husband's orders: the kingpin wanted his top aide to immediately start the process of bribing the guards at Altiplano. It was a task to which Damaso was particularly suited. Long before he had joined the ranks of the Company's upper management, Damaso had served as a deputy warden at the Puente Grande prison, in charge of its security when Guzmán was there serving his initial prison term. The two men, almost from the moment of their meeting, saw an opportunity for mutual advantage. Whenever the prisoner needed something—an illegal cell phone or a visit from one of his wives—the deputy warden provided it. Damaso, in exchange, received small gifts of gratitude: boxes of money or a brand-new house in town.

Better than anyone, perhaps, Damaso understood the ways in which the staff at Altiplano might be softened, and assured the boss's wife that she could count on his assistance. Within a few days, he delegated the task of paying off the guards to one of his own brothers-in-law. Presumably, with a wad of dirty cash.

---

cians in Emma's hometown. The groom wore blue jeans; the bride turned eighteen. The municipal police were kind enough to close the local roads surrounding the event to uninvited guests. The only excitement came the following day when soldiers from the Ninth Military Zone showed up for a raid—hours after the newlyweds had already slipped away.

*   *   *

Once the breakout plot was underway, Guzmán had little else to do but wait and returned to the details of running the Company's business. Most of this business was handled in letters to Damaso, delivered through the spring by the lawyer, Oscar Gomez.

It had always been the kingpin's plan for Damaso to take control of the Company's operations in his absence, and now he drowned his chief of staff in a flood of endless tasks. In the letters, Damaso was instructed to keep close watch on various policemen, pay the rents for his European front companies and be certain that the widows of any murdered hit men received their regular stipends. "The crop-duster should be started and flown so that it doesn't get ruined," Guzmán wrote. "Cachimba and Capi Cesar know where it is."

In between these petty requests, there was a darker, more disturbing agenda. Alone in his cell at Altiplano, the kingpin, inclined toward paranoia, was searching for the turncoat who had led to his arrest. He soon became obsessed with the idea that his organization was riddled with informants. His suspicions, roving wide, grew to include his local team in Ecuador, his top man in Honduras, even one of his closest friends: Alex Cifuentes. Alex had been sent to Altiplano following his own arrest in late 2013, and a few days after arriving at the prison, Guzmán had encountered him in the yard. Their meeting did not go well. Alex's older brother, Jorge, had by then also been arrested and was in American custody, and Guzmán walked away from his exchange with Alex convinced that both men were going to betray him. Not long after seeing Alex, he wrote another letter to Damaso, nervously alerting him to beware of "fingers"—traitors—and asking him to look after his four sons.

There are two things that must be done: No one should know where you all sleep and don't go to public places. . . . The dan-

ger is the people from the Company, because they're the ones
who know about you, and they're the ones who can set you up.
The five of you should talk about what I'm telling you. . . . Like
I said, without a "finger," they will never find you. . . . And a
"finger" will always be someone close to us.

Guzmán, in the end, let Alex go with a warning. ("I told him to
keep his mouth shut," he later wrote Damaso.) But he was not so lib-
eral with another close aide who had also lost his trust: Bravo Aponte,
his plaza boss in Mazatlán. Aponte, a former soldier who had served
the kingpin for a decade, had failed the boss in an irredeemable
fashion. After receiving Guzmán on the highway from Picudo, his
counterpart in Culiacán, Aponte had been charged with protecting
Guzmán in Mazatlán where the arrest had taken place. It was often
difficult to understand how Guzmán decided who would live and
who would die. But some combination of Aponte's lapse and his own
mounting anxieties pushed him over the edge.

In early April, the kingpin reached out to Damaso again, this time
instructing him to ask Mayo Zambada to assassinate Aponte. A few
days later, the police in Sinaloa found the body. Aponte had been
shot six times and was dumped beneath a fence outside a factory in
La Cruz de Elota, a small town on the western coastline that he had
known so well. [31]

*   *   *

31. When Guzmán later learned that Alex was determined to betray him and was
planning to talk with the American authorities, he was far less easygoing. First, he had
a lawyer approach Alex, offering to give him control of an innovative smuggling route
the Company had devised: moving drugs on medevac flights of burn victims from
Mexico to a hospital in Texas. Then, when Alex refused the deal and was moved from
Altiplano to a prison in Colombia, the kingpin contrived to sneak a quantity of C-4
plastic explosives into Alex's cell in a plot to blow him up.

By late May 2014, the conspirators had finalized their plans.

Guzmán's sons had now joined the plot and, working in tandem with Oscar Gomez's straw men, they started to look for land near Altiplano, close enough to the prison to be useful, but not so close as to attract unwanted scrutiny. They soon had several options, mostly small *ranchitos* and derelict industrial spreads that may have once been used by the region's farmers. In his usual role as supervisor, Damaso was asked to be sure there was a structure on whatever property was finally acquired that was large enough to hide the signs of the construction they were planning. It would not have surprised anyone involved that the project's engineer, Lazaro Araujo Burgos, was proposing to build a tunnel.

Guzmán had been using tunnels since the early 1990s for a variety of purposes: to store his merchandise, to move it under borders and, of course, to accomplish his escapes. Araujo was only the latest tunnel maker in a long line that reached back to Felipe Corona-Verbera, who had built the tunnel underneath the pool table near the Arizona border; and José Sánchez-Villalobos, whose own projects largely ran from Tijuana to San Diego.[32] But Araujo's job, while similar to those of his predecessors, was constrained by certain technical demands. His central challenge was to get his crew of diggers, working underground, to cut their way in a more or less straight line directly into the shower of Guzmán's cell—the only place that he was not surveilled by Altiplano's cameras. It was likely that Araujo himself came up with a solution to the problem. The breakout team was told to find a watch with a GPS application and to sneak it into the prison past the guards.

---

32. Corona-Verbera was convicted at trial in Arizona in 2006 and sentenced to eighteen years in prison. Shortly after being indicted in San Diego in 2012, Sánchez-Villalobos was arrested by the Mexican police in Zapopan, Jalisco. He was imprisoned at Altiplano at the same time Guzmán was there, prompting speculation that he might have helped consult on Araujo's tunnel project from within the facility itself. In January 2020, he was extradited to stand trial in the United States.

"We had to buy it and to get it in . . . to get the coordinates from the cell where my *compadre* was," Damaso later said.

Over the summer, the plotters met to update one another on their progress. Guzmán had by that point received the watch. His sons, meanwhile, had closed on a piece of real estate: a cinderblock warehouse in a weed-strewn lot in Santa Juanita, a village in the flatlands in sight of Altiplano. When Araujo's tunnel rats moved in, they erected an outbuilding, sleeping on the floors, cooking in the makeshift kitchen and installing heavy equipment—chiefly, an air compressor that would run the tunnel's ventilation system. The compressor was housed in the basement of the warehouse, its exhaust pipes funneled through a gas-powered grill outside in the yard.

All told, it was nearly a mile from the tunnel's entrance in the warehouse to its terminus in Guzmán's cell, a distance that required as many as a dozen men at least ten months to quarry. Evidenced by what was left behind—jackhammers, spades, bed litters, oxygen tanks, hydraulic fluid, shoring timbers, steel-mesh coils, .45-caliber pistols and a few unopened beers in the fridge—the work was likely grueling. Little by little, the crew scratched forward, chipping at the soil and stone and slowly hauling out nearly three thousand tons of earthen debris. To quicken the excavation, the team set up a winch with a heavy-duty cable; and to ensure their own safety, they mounted lengths of PVC pipe on the ceiling to rig the site with fresh air from a blower. Fluorescent bulbs were attached to the pipes to bring in light, and a crude metal track was bolted to the ground. Along the track ran the project's most ingenious innovation—an ersatz railcar powered by the stripped-down frame of a cheap imported motorbike.

At a final meeting, in mid-2015, Emma brought word to the escape team that her husband wanted to bring things to a head on Saturday, July 4. It would be wonderful, he had told her, to embarrass the Americans on their most important holiday. He had also determined that on summer weekends, the prison was understaffed and there were no official visits from court personnel that might bring extra bodies into the compound.

But the tunnel wasn't ready in time and the plotters decided to delay the operation by a week. By then, Emma was reporting, Guzmán could hear the sounds of the construction near his cell. The kingpin's eldest sons did not believe her; but then, the two boys, Iván and Alfredo, knew as much about building tunnels as they did about conducting secret missions. A few months earlier, even as the digging crew was still underground, Iván had gone onto Twitter and boasted to the world, "I promise you the general will be back soon." It was a reckless breach of security, one that he made worse just days before the planned escape when he posted another tweet:

"Everything comes for those who know how to wait."

After waiting for a year and a half, the solitary inmate in Cell 20 in Corridor 2 of the Altiplano prison appeared in normal spirits. It was the evening of July 11, 2015, and to anyone observing him—as certainly they were—it would have seemed like any other Saturday night in summer. The prisoner, in his jailhouse pajamas, was stretched out full beneath the covers of his bunk. He was watching TV from a tablet on the nightstand, cradling a pillow at his head.

The show that he had on—presumably a comedy of some sort—was full of raucous laughter and applause. But even with the volume turned up high, it was not enough to muffle the racket of what seemed to be a hammer pounding under the floor beneath his shower stall. Looking mildly curious, like a man who had heard a dog bark in the night, he pushed back his blanket and got out of bed to investigate the sound.

For the next few minutes, he was on his feet walking back and forth in a manner that was, as an official report would later note, "the natural behavior of inmates." After further pacing and a quick stop on the bed to change his shoes, he rose again and returned to the shower: this time, he crouched down behind its low half-wall.

As the laughter cackled from the tablet on his nightstand, Guzmán dropped into the small hole that had been cut in the shower floor. And with that maneuver, he was gone.

Twenty-six minutes later—at 9:18 p.m.—a guard showed up outside his empty cell.

"Guzmán?" he called. "Guzmán? Guzmán Loera? Can you hear me?"

When no one responded, the guard reached for his radio and alerted his commander.

Commandante, can you hear me?
What happened?
There is a hole in the shower.
What?
There is a hole in the shower.
There is a hole?
Confirmed, confirmed. In the . . . in the drain of the shower, there is a hole.
What size is it?
Very big, Commandante. Big . . .
But is the inmate there?
No, Commandante, he is not.

After ducking through the hole, Guzmán had clambered down a thirty-foot ladder. At the bottom of the ladder, he was met by Emma's brother Edgar Coronel. Edgar ferried him to safety, taking the controls of the motorcycle railcar as Guzmán rode in front of him on the platform. Rushing forward through the bulb-lit darkness, they made their way toward the tunnel's exit in the warehouse. There, the kingpin slipped out of his prison clothes, grabbed a weapon and hopped aboard a waiting ATV.

After that, there was a brief ride to a second warehouse, where the fugitive was hidden in the trailer of a truck for the two-hour drive on local roads to San Juan del Rio, Querétaro. On the outskirts of the city was a fumigation airstrip; and on the airstrip were two small planes, fueled and ready for takeoff. One of the planes was a decoy, meant to distract pursuers. But the other, manned by Cachimba, the kingpin's favorite pilot, sailed into the night.

Forty minutes later, the red alert went out at Altiplano.

But by that point, Guzmán was already en route to his home in the Sierras and a mountaintop encampment called The Sky.

TEN

The High Side

July 2015–January 2016

Donovan's wife woke him in the morning with the news. Half asleep, he dismissed it as a joke.

"Get up," her words came through to him as a hand pushed at his shoulder. "Ray, get up. Chapo just escaped."

Sure, he thought, *escaped, you're hilarious*. But the hand kept pushing until he heard a sound that might have been the sound of his phone going crazy on the nightstand. Rolling over, he saw that there were panicked texts from Washington, Virginia, Mexico City. The TV, when he turned it on, was worse. There it was on cable, every anchor in America discussing the destruction of his life's achievement. Sick to his stomach, Donovan hadn't even had his morning cup of coffee yet. "It was total turmoil," he recalled. "The biggest thing in my career and now it's a complete disaster."[33]

---

33. Bob Potash had a similar experience. He was on vacation with his wife down south, a work moratorium in effect, when his phone started buzzing at six in the morning. It

Back in the office that first day, Donovan monitored developments on the ground. The Mexicans were going crazy, mobilizing anyone in a uniform, down to the Boy Scouts, it appeared. Hundreds of federal highway cops had set up checkpoints near the prison and on all roads leading from Toluca into neighboring states. More police had taken over toll booths and set up posts in three different airports in the region. The army had surrounded Altiplano, and the navy had sent its own troops to the area from more than a dozen bases. Marine commandos on both coasts of the country had been placed on high alert.

Promoted after his accomplishments in Mazatlán, Donovan was now in charge of SOD's entire Mexican section, which meant that it was his responsibility to figure out what the hell had happened down there. Admittedly, even with Guzmán's prior history, he hadn't given too much thought to the chance of another escape. Once, he figured, maybe. But *twice*? And from the country's most secure federal prison? The general consensus in Chantilly had always been that Guzmán would eventually stand trial in the United States. His extradition would no doubt be delayed by the usual legal wrangling, but everyone at SOD believed that in another few years, the kingpin would be flown up to New York or Chicago and it would be done for good. Donovan had not lost sight completely of the happenings in Mexico; he had kept loose tabs on the politics and the lawyerly maneuvers. But along the way, he soon discovered, he had missed something. As part of his new job, he had recently pitched in on a field office wiretap in Tucson that was surveilling some of Mayo Zambada's men. Among the messages the wire had intercepted were a few obscure mentions of a warehouse that one of Guzmán's own crews had been building. When Donovan went back to check the line sheets, it was obvious in hindsight that

---

was a colleague from New York, texting to say that Guzmán had escaped. When his wife asked what was going on, Potash told her; at first, she did not believe him. It took googling "Chapo" and "escape" to persuade her. The rest of the day was in ruins.

the targets of the wire had been talking about the warehouse outside Altiplano. Though he and his colleagues had no way of knowing it at the time, Sinaloa had planned the escape directly under their eyes.

Slumped behind his desk at SOD, Donovan realized he had a choice to make: He could either accept defeat and let the Mexicans fix the mess or he could suck up yet another failure and—hard to believe that he was thinking this—do it all again. Whether it was the burdens of promotion, or a kind of self-inflicted castigation, or simply an obsession with the man who had slipped his grasp, he decided by the end of the week to put the coalition back together. At that point, there was only one question: Who was going to join in the pursuit this second time?

Drew Hogan, in a blaze of burned bridges, had already left the DEA's embassy office to start work on a book. Victor Vazquez had gone off as well, to a new assignment in Arizona. But Brian Maxwell was still in Mexico and the Narco Polo team was still in San Diego. Donovan, knowing they were fellow Guzmán zealots, was able to recruit them to his team.

After the kingpin's last arrest, in February 2014, Jake Healy, from Homeland Security Investigations, had left Nogales for Washington, DC. There had been threats that Guzmán's sons were coming after him and other law enforcement agents working on the border. Though Healy's wiretap had largely been dismantled, he had been working with the Justice Department, which had finally indicted several of his targets, among them Speedy, Omega and Rincon, the kingpin's operative in Ecuador.[34]

When Healy got Donovan's offer to work at SOD and finish what

---

34. Speedy (Ulises Betanzos Diego), Omega (Edgar Javier Gonzalez Campean) and the Ecuadorean operative Rincon (Hector Coronel Castillo) were all indicted by the Justice Department in the District of Columbia. In early 2020, each of their cases remained under seal.

they started, he accepted. He brought along Nick Nordstrom, one of his partners from Nogales.

As the team came together, Donovan was still in need of an intelligence machine to replace the shut-down wire in Nogales. For that, he turned to two new faces, both of them from New York. Fernando Cruz, a hulking man with the unlikely nickname Fern, was one of the DEA's top data nerds, a technical savant with a gift for crunching numbers to crack communications systems. Based on Long Island, Cruz had for years been chasing Mayo Zambada, most recently with Michael Robotti, a tall, lanky prosecutor working out of Brooklyn. Now that Guzmán was at large again, Donovan sought to reorient their talents. "We needed records and data," he said, "because without the intel, we were dead in the water. Michael was the most aggressive prosecutor in the country, a monster in the most respectful way. And Fern was the perfect match, relentless and totally committed."

With a second coalition now in place, all that Donovan needed was a code name for his mission. After the swing-and-miss in Cabo and the vexing foul tip of the escape, this attempt, he hoped, would be the final pitch at Guzmán.

He called the operation Third Strike.

Before it began in earnest that summer, Donovan added one more weapon to his arsenal. It was a secret weapon, discussed in whispers even inside SOD: the National Security Agency.

Since its founding in 1952, the NSA had been the country's foremost collector of signals, or communications, intelligence. Based at an army base in Fort Meade, Maryland, forty minutes from Washington, DC, it was even more clandestine than the CIA: its initials, people joked, stood for No Such Agency. In July 2015, as Operation Third Strike was getting underway, the NSA was still recovering from the scandal that had broken out two years earlier when Edward Snowden, a former contractor, leaked thousands of secret documents suggesting that its spies had engaged in a pattern of illegal surveillance on American citizens. Donovan had approached the agency cautiously at first. But after several meetings—some of them over crab cakes at a local Maryland seafood joint—he came to admire the spooks and analysts who worked within its walls.[35]

With its traditional ties to the intelligence community, SOD had been working on the Guzmán case with the spies at NSA in one form or another since at least 2012, tracking the kingpin's movements and occasionally snooping on his chats and conversations through warrantless surveillance from what was known in law enforcement circles as the "high side." Even during the heyday of the wiretap machine, Donovan had availed himself of the agency's secret listening techniques. At that point, the NSA's efforts had been somewhat less essential: the "low side," or court-approved, intercepts that Donovan was getting from Nogales, San Diego, Chicago and New York were already so numerous and rich with information that he didn't need much off-the-books assistance. Throughout 2013, as the coalition mapped the kingpin's network and cracked the Office system, the NSA had been helpful mostly as a backstop, monitoring Guzmán and his allies when and in ways the low-side listeners could not. After Duck Dynasty, when things got operational and sped up on the ground, the spooks became more central in the chase.

The thing was, Fort Meade's spies were fast. If the coalition needed something on the fly, the NSA could get it. But what the high side had in speed, it lacked in understanding. Its analysts were nowhere near as skilled at deciphering the Office's coded chats as the wiretap readers

---

35. Donovan declined to discuss the NSA's involvement in the case, but several other people confirmed it. The NSA itself responded to a Freedom of Information Act request about its role in hunting Guzmán with a standard letter of denial. "We have determined," the letter said, "that the fact of the existence or non-existence of the materials you request is a currently and properly classified matter."

in Nogales, who had all spent months immersed in the cartel's BBM texts and had developed an instinctive feeling for the diction and the habits of their targets. Under Donovan's guidance, the spies and agents in the first operation had worked on separate but symbiotic tracks. Staying in their own lanes, they harmonized the gathering of evidence that could be used to prove their case against the kingpin with the collection of intelligence that could lead to his arrest.

"Ray embraced the idea that different people could help at different times," one member of the coalition said. "It was like a baseball team. One guy is good at hitting curves. Another guy is good at hitting fastballs. It's good to have both guys in the lineup side by side."

By the time Third Strike was launched, Donovan had placed the high-side hitters at the heart of his new lineup. This was a decision matching tactical abilities with circumstantial realities. With Guzmán on the run again, speed was of the essence. There was also no real need this time to collect more evidence; the Arizona wiretap alone had vacuumed up more than a million intercepts, sufficient proof to convict the kingpin and dozens of his allies ten times over.

In Third Strike's sleeker world, a new working paradigm emerged. Donovan and his team at SOD—"Digging, digging, digging," as he put it—collected BlackBerry PINs from anywhere they could find them: the remnants of Drew Hogan's work, the Mexican authorities investigating Guzmán's escape, confidential informants and dormant lines from Nogales. Once they had those BlackBerry PINs, Fernando Cruz would send them on to Brooklyn, where Mike Robotti, the prosecutorial monster, worked around the clock to get judicial permission to examine their call records. The records were then sent back to Cruz, who leaned into the data and determined which devices were the "hottest"—or seemed like nodes on the network. Some of the hot phones were forwarded to Fort Meade for secret interception. Summaries of the intercepts were often returned to SOD, where Healy and Nordstrom, skilled wire readers, struggled to interpret and make sense of them.

This new machine, designed to hunt, was infinitely quicker than the old one, and within a matter of weeks the coalition had hacked back into the pyramid of mirrors. Donovan and his team hadn't spied on Guzmán in more than a year, but eavesdropping on the kingpin and his entourage was not unlike tuning in to the second season of a good TV show. All of the familiar players had returned. There was Damaso López, holding things together as he always did; and there was Cachimba, the kingpin's favorite pilot. Emma Coronel, Guzmán's wife, was still in the picture, and so was much of the rambling support cast of doctors, lawyers, accountants, cooks and finance guys.

As with any good TV show, there were a few new characters too—or rather, those who had stepped from the background of the story into more important roles. Cholo Ivan, the impulsive killer from Los Mochis, was back this season playing what appeared to be a larger part as Guzmán's top security chief. In an unexpected twist, Lucero Sánchez, the kingpin's mistress, had run for public office and was now serving as an elected representative in the Sinaloa congress. Many of the intercepts suggested that Guzmán himself had once again holed up in his stronghold in the mountains in between his home state and its neighboring state, Durango. That meant that his brother Aureliano, who was based nearby, had also become more prominent this time and was roaming the countryside, protecting Guzmán with scores of local gunmen.

After getting the early readouts Donovan noticed something, though. It seemed Fort Meade was picking up a steady stream of messages flowing up the pyramid from all the usual places—Guzmán's sons, his girlfriends, the aides who brought his food—but wasn't seeing answers coming back down in the opposite direction. The Top Tier of the pyramid—Guzmán's tier, that is—appeared to be hidden in a void. Donovan could see the void, the contours of its emptiness, and they were troubling. The void suggested something ominous had happened: the kingpin had traded in his old devices for fully encrypted Blackphones.[36]

It had to be the tech team, Donovan thought, or even worse, Chaneke. The tech team was bad enough. When Christian Rodriguez fled his job with Guzmán in late 2012, other techies, like Charly Martinez, had taken his place. Building on the young Colombian's work, Martinez could easily have made possible the sudden switch to Blackphones, which would have pleased Chaneke, the kingpin's latest bodyguard, who had taken over after Condor was arrested at the Miramar. A countersurveillance expert, Chaneke was exceptionally cagey, changing his own phones constantly and avoiding signature monikers like Condor's helicopter models. It would have been exactly like Chaneke to have requisitioned new phones that even the spooks at the NSA were having trouble cracking. The coalition hated Chaneke. Chaneke was smart and he didn't make mistakes.

Wherever Guzmán was—in a hilltop hut, an encampment in the forest or hiding in a cave in a narrow mountain valley—if he was with Chaneke, finding him was going to be a chore.

In Mexico, however, Brian Maxwell had just found Chaneke. The bodyguard and his boss, B-Max had discovered, had garrisoned themselves with a company of gunmen at a small ranch in the dense jungle wilderness twenty miles outside Cosalá, Lucero Sánchez's hometown.

From the start of Operation Third Strike, Maxwell had been in the

---

36. Blackphones, made by the Swiss company Silent Circle, were the cutting edge of encryption technology. With their complicated software, Blackphones far surpassed both Guzmán's standard BlackBerries and Christian Rodriguez's Nokias in providing secure communications.

field again, traveling with the Mexican Marines. But the Marines in 2015 were not the same Marines they had been the year before. In the months since Guzmán's last arrest, the professional commando unit, which had always been skilled in tactical maneuvers, had greatly enhanced its intelligence capacity. Much like SOD had struck up a relationship with the spies at the NSA, the Marines had forged a partnership with their own country's spies at the intelligence service, CISEN.

The inner workings of any secret agency can be nebulous at best, but every now and then the coalition heard things. Recently they had picked up whispers about a covert wiretap that CISEN had been running from its own perch on the high side. The managers of the CISEN wire, or so the whispers said, had focused their attention on certain Mexican political officials suspected of helping Guzmán in the weeks and months that preceded his escape. One of the wire's targets was the newly elected politician Lucero Sánchez. Some of Guzmán's lawyers and his trusted pilot, Cachimba, had been targeted as well.[37]

Imagine, then, the embarrassment CISEN must have felt when Guzmán managed to escape in spite of this surveillance. The disconnected threads of the plot were right there in its wiretap recordings, ready to be tied together and prevented—if anyone had noticed them in time. The situation, while undeniably awkward, at least had an upside. If the spies at CISEN now resolved to go after Guzmán quickly, all they had to do was pass the information they had gleaned from

---

37. At its height, the CISEN wire was tracking more than a dozen targets, and the kingpin himself was identified in the intercepts by one of the wiretap's more hilarious episodes. During his stint in prison, while Guzmán's family was living near Altiplano, his two young daughters acquired a pet monkey named Boots. After the kingpin escaped from prison and the family rushed to join him in the mountains, moving to a small town near Tamazula, Durango, Boots was left behind. Guzmán's daughters missed their pet and prevailed upon their father to send a group of men to fetch him. The Mexican intelligence service recorded Guzmán delivering orders to bring him the monkey in the mountains, helping to confirm his location. The Mexican spies wanted at one point to place a tracking device on Boots, but in the end were unable to pull it off.

their wire to their new collaborators, the Mexican Marines, who were already working with Maxwell's snatch-and-grab team. It would not be easy to find the kingpin in all that highland jungle. But with a basic location provided by the wire—the village of Cosalá—and the right equipment—a cell-site simulator, flown in an airplane at the proper height and speed—it was only a matter of time.

Donovan was impressed. He had noticed from the outset of Third Strike that the Mexicans were on their game in this iteration of the chase in a way that they had never been before. Every time the co-alition developed a new lead, his counterparts in Mexico already seemed to be on to it. Eventually he learned how they had managed the trick. Aside from its wiretap, CISEN had a second secret weapon: a classified Israeli technology called Pegasus.

Pegasus—created by the NSO Group, a tech firm based near Tel Aviv—accomplished what appeared to be an impossible task. It broke into even the most encrypted phones remotely and, milliseconds before the data housed in them was encoded, stole it without leaving a trace. Nothing was safe from the system's prying fingers: phone calls, texts, emails, even chats on Facebook, Skype and WhatsApp could be pilfered. Though the software was devilishly intricate, the way it penetrated phones was relatively simple. NSO would send its targets innocent-looking texts or emails, known as Trojan horses, and as soon as the messages were opened, the malware was installed. Pega-sus was expensive: NSO charged its clients each time it was used. But by spending cautiously, the operatives at CISEN were able to map out Guzmán's Blackphone network, one phone at a time.

In late September, armed with CISEN's intelligence, the Marines went into training, preparing to raid the ranch outside Cosalá. There was every indication it was going to take a fight. The mountain prop-erty was little more than a smattering of huts, but Guzmán and his soldiers had fortified themselves beneath the lush woodland cover.

As the day of the assault—October 2—neared, Donovan was filled with anxious pride. It was a huge accomplishment that only weeks after Third Strike had begun, the Marines were getting ready to attack. He and the coalition were getting ready too. In preparation for the raid on Cosalá, they arranged to put a drone in the air above the ranch with a live feed piped into Chantilly.

The team at SOD would get to watch.

The day before the raid went off, Donovan got an email.

Sitting at his desk in Virginia, he saw it had come from a colleague at Customs who was writing to alert him that one of the subjects of his Chapo Guzmán case was about to leave an airport in Van Nuys, California, on a private jet for Mexico. The subject in question, the Mexican actress Kate del Castillo, was, according to the flight report, traveling with three other passengers. Scrolling through the email, Donovan clocked two of the passengers as Argentinian film producers. The third, however, was an American—and a disaster. It was the actor Sean Penn.

Donovan was familiar—all too familiar by then—with the strange events that had placed the star in the middle of his capture operation. Earlier that winter, while Guzmán was still in prison, he had asked his lawyers—including Oscar Gomez, who was planning his escape—to contact del Castillo with yet another plea to make his movie, and she had finally relented. The project, at that stage, had been in turnaround for nearly a year; everyone associated with it was either in custody, as Guzmán was himself, or was running from the kingpin for their lives. Apparently unaware that her new business partner had tried to kill both his writer, Javier Rey, and Andrea Velez, the assistant he had assigned to the project, del Castillo reached an agreement with the kingpin to buy his life rights with the two Argentinians, Fernando Sulichin and José Ibáñez. After Guzmán escaped from Altiplano and was front-page news for days, Sean Penn joined the team. While del Castillo was convinced that the involvement of a Hollywood celebrity would make the film more viable, Penn was noncommittal. He was, however, interested in meeting Guzmán, having made his own arrangements to interview the kingpin for *Rolling Stone* magazine.

Third Strike intersected with this three-ring circus not long after the operation started. Near the end of September 2015, two months after Guzmán's escape, del Castillo flew to Guadalajara, ostensibly for the birthday party of a friend, but also to meet with Guzmán's lawyers. The coalition had been spying on the lawyers for weeks and intercepted the actress chatting, through them, with their boss. Using the same filter-based communications system he had devised to make his drug deals, the kingpin asked the actress to join him at a ranch near Mazatlán to discuss their pending deal. Del Castillo, sounding starstruck, accepted the invitation.

9:55 P.M.: Amiga . . . I really want to meet you and become good friends. You are the best of this world. . . . I will take care of you more than I do my own eyes.

10:11 P.M.: It moves me so much that you say you'll take care of me—nobody has ever taken care of me, thank you! And I'll be free next weekend!

Once they set a date—October 2—del Castillo went back to her party. The lawyers stayed on the line and Guzmán ordered them to buy the actress a BlackBerry so that they could chat in private—a pink one, if they could find it. When the lawyers told the boss that del Castillo was planning to bring not only the Argentinians but Sean Penn too—"One of the most recognized actors in Hollywood"—Guzmán admitted he had never heard of Penn. Searching his filmography on Google, one of the lawyers reported that Penn was the star of *21 Grams* and had directed *The Pledge* and *The Crossing Guard*—both of which, he pointed out, had featured Jack Nicholson. Within a few hours, Guzmán himself had looked up Penn on Google. He was sold.

All of this was so insane that even now, with the Marines in place outside Cosalá, Donovan had no idea what to make of it. He was not alone in his bafflement. Other members of the coalition had taken their reports on the del Castillo intercepts into the so-called SCIF at SOD, a secure facility for classified material, and come out looking mystified and ashen. The absurdity was overwhelming, veering off in a dozen different directions. It was undeniably mental that the NSA—*the NSA*—had used its secret hardware to eavesdrop on the world's most wanted criminal vetting Sean Penn's Hollywood career. And yet it was in keeping with Guzmán's schizophrenic world. After being privy for nearly three years to the most intimate aspects of the kingpin's life, Donovan wasn't surprised. "It all goes back to how his mind works," he said. "Kate was in touch with him when he was still in prison. But now that he was out, he was a big man again. He's always been the same—arrogant, cocky, narcissistic. He wanted to be bigger than Escobar. He wanted to tell his story."

Seconds after reading the email from Customs, Donovan was on the phone to the embassy in Mexico. Working up the chain of command, he finally got the DEA's regional director on the line. "Look," he said, "Sean Penn's going to be there. I don't know if we can launch." Donovan wasn't sure if they should still do the op; he wasn't sure if they *could* still do the op. Maybe, he said, they should scrub it or delay it. The regional director promised to get back to him after speaking with the Mexicans.

The real issue, Donovan understood, was not Sean Penn. The real issue was that SOD was certain—given what it knew about Guzmán—that he would never bring his visitors to the place where he was hiding. Instead, it was assumed, he would leave the property near Cosalá and meet them somewhere else. And that, to put it lightly, would be challenging since the strike team of Marines had already spent days practicing maneuvers designed to hit that ranch.

When the embassy got back to him, Donovan was stunned to hear that the Marines still wanted to go forward. After all their training, he was told, their attitude appeared to be: *Fuck Sean Penn, the raid goes on as planned.* At that point, there wasn't much that he, or any other American, could do. The Mexicans were in charge of operations on the ground and had been tracking Penn and del Castillo from the moment that their jet touched down at the Guadalajara airport. Under surveillance, the actors and their Argentinian partners had gone to their hotel, dropped off their belongings and then, escorted by the kingpin's men, were driven to a nearby airstrip where they boarded a pair of Cessnas. That's when things had threatened to go off the rails. As they all took off, the Marines had abruptly improvised a new plan. They wanted to follow the actors to Guzmán's mountain compound and send in the Black Hawks underneath the cover of their planes.

Squelching that idea led to an uproarious, international shouting match, which nearly rose to the level of a diplomatic incident. "It was complete and total panic—a living shitshow," one member of the coalition said. "No one, nobody, knew what to do."

In the end, the kingpin and the weather took control of the situation. Guzmán, as expected, left his ranch outside Cosalá and met the stars in a much less compromising setting: a darkly wooded patch of the University of Sinaloa's ecology reserve. But even if he had stayed put, the raid would still have been impossible. Late that night, a storm blew through the mountains with sheets of monsoon rain and "great bolts of lightning . . . like flash-bang grenades," as Penn would later write. The strike team's Black Hawks never left the ground.

*   *   *

Four days later, when the skies were clear and the visitors were gone, the Marines tried again. It was now October 6 and daybreak in Cosalá. At SOD headquarters, Donovan and his team gathered around a monitor. The drone was in the air this time and they watched the operation through its feed.

Their pixilated live screen showed the muddle of the skirmish: First, the helicopters wheeling toward the little mountain clearing and then the bursts of phosphorescent gunfire streaking toward the sky. As the Black Hawks hovered, some of the kingpin's men began to scatter, and after that it was chaos. Donovan could see the hazy shapes of ATVs racing through the compound and the splotches of the strike team descending their rappelling lines. But at a distance, in the disarray of vehicles and bodies, it was hard to tell what was happening on the ground. Guzmán, he was later told, had holed up during the worst of the fighting with his cooks and one of their children, protected by a handful of his gunmen. Then, as the Marines fanned out, kicking down doors and taking over buildings, he had ducked into the bush and slipped away.

Ten days later, he was still on the run. On each of those excruciating mornings, when Donovan got to work, there might, if he was lucky, be an update. Kept in the loop by Maxwell in the field and by a liaison at the embassy in Mexico, he knew that after losing sight of Guzmán the Marines had tried to pen him in by encircling Cosalá. They had dropped a ring of roadblocks on the mountain byways in an iron net from Tamazula to Verano. Scouring the countryside on foot and in the air, they were stopping pickup trucks, breaking into houses and rounding up farmers believed to have been sheltering the kingpin. But as the search went on from house to house and from town to town, the troops were getting nowhere and hundreds of local residents, displaced by the violence, were starting to get angry. Some of the refugees had gone to the media, complaining about their frightened children and their bullet-ridden windows. *They shot our homes,* they said, *they torched our cars.* The Marines, it was true, could be brutal. But the coalition also suspected that Lucero Sánchez, the district's representative, was quietly behind the publicity campaign.

From a tactical perspective, the Cosalá mission was becoming unsustainable. Inside the villages, the residents were terrified. Outside the villages, the rocky brush and deep pine forest were impenetrable. Moving in between the villages, the Marines were exposed to constant attacks from Guzmán's brother Aureliano and another local warlord known as Memo. Some of these attacks, Donovan heard in exhausted calls with Maxwell, were even more ferocious than the first one in Cosalá. They were full-scale battles with men on four-wheel buggies firing machine guns and shoulder-mounted rockets.

Donovan needed a break. But stuck at SOD, there was little he could do. Maxwell was calling several times a day with BlackBerry PINs seized from prisoners they had taken. Working with Mike Robotti, Fernando Cruz secured their call logs and squeezed the PINs for information, looking for a pattern, a digital map, that could point them toward the phones that Guzmán and Chaneke might be using. But as the data came back, there didn't seem to be a pattern—or much of a map. Before the raid in Cosalá, they had at least seen the void at the Top Tier of the pyramid. Now it all seemed like a void.

The break came just as a deep mood of gloom threatened to consume SOD. Maxwell called one day to report that the Marines had captured a crew of Guzmán's lookouts. The lookouts had been using simple radios. But when Maxwell and his team listened to the radios, they heard transmissions describing what appeared to be a new communications system: encrypted walkie-talkies. These walkie-talkies weren't just standard portable devices. They seemed to be connected to a large, private Wi-Fi network boosted through the mountains by a series of repeaters.

Maxwell recognized the method: Guzmán's enemies, the Zetas, had used something similar for a decade. When he tracked the signal and hacked into the walkie-talkie network, he discovered good news. According to the chatter, Guzmán had fallen in Cosalá and broken one of his legs. With the boss severely hobbled, Chaneke and Cholo Ivan, his new security chief, had been hauling him through the wilderness on anything they could find: donkeys, rafts and all-terrain vehicles.

Donovan allowed himself a glimmer of excitement. How far could Guzmán get—could anybody get—with a broken leg on donkey-back?

Another day, however, brought more chatter on the walkie-talkies: The two lieutenants and their injured boss had managed to slip the military cordon.

They were gone.

No one could believe it. But there it was, not only in the encrypted walkie-talkie runs, but in corroborating intercepts from Pegasus. Soon the Mexicans had more bad news to report. After ducking the Marine perimeter, Guzmán and Chaneke had made their way back to the kingpin's birthplace in La Tuna.

Three hundred miles to the north, La Tuna sat in a swath of the Sierras that was arguably more remote and treacherous than Cosalá. Filled with farmers and ranchers he had known his entire life, it was also more familiar and friendlier terrain. Not long after arriving in La Tuna, Guzmán it appeared had settled in at one of his ranches, surrounded by an army captained by his brother, who was based in the region's municipal seat in Badiraguato. He was comfortable enough up there that he reached out again to Kate del Castillo.

10:15 P.M.: Amiga, we must see each other. Everything will be calm. If I wasn't sure, I wouldn't invite you. I want you to interview the men and women of my ranch. . . . My mom wants to meet you. I told her about you.

If the Mexican assessments were correct, Guzmán had gone native in La Tuna. By late October, the intercepts from Pegasus were suggesting something straight out of Osama bin Laden's playbook. The kingpin and Chaneke had, it seemed, started to split their time between the ranch in La Tuna and a kind of mountain cave, miles from the nearest human settlement. There wasn't much of an appetite to head into the wilderness and get them. If going into Culiacán had been like going into the lion's den, trekking into the woods around La Tuna would be like walking naked into the savanna.

But there was a different option. Recently the spies at CISEN and the NSA had been picking up indications that Guzmán was building a house in Los Mochis, a sweaty little beach town a few hours north of Culiacán. Donovan was intrigued by the project. Los Mochis was the stronghold of Cholo Ivan, the kingpin's chief of security. Two more of Guzmán's top men seemed to be in charge of the construction of the house. One of them was an engineer nicknamed La Quinta who had designed several tunnels for the kingpin and had managed the development of his refuge at Duck Dynasty. The other was Charly Martinez, Christian Rodriguez's protégé on the tech team.

With talent like that involved, the house had to be more than just a house: it had to be a safe house. And there was only one reason why Guzmán would be building another safe house now. He wanted to leave La Tuna for Los Mochis.[38]

The high side now turned its attention to La Quinta and Martinez. Once both CISEN and the NSA homed in on them, finding the house was relatively easy.

By mid-November 2015, an undercover unit of Marines was quietly posted at the white two-story structure, which sat in the heart of Las Palmas, one of Los Mochis's wealthiest residential neighborhoods. From the outside it seemed normal, sitting on a peaceful street

---

38. It has never been explained why Guzmán wanted to leave his sanctuary in the mountains for Los Mochis. Perhaps he trusted the work of La Quinta more than the natural protections of La Tuna. Perhaps he felt that Cholo Ivan would be able to protect him. Perhaps, as in Los Cabos, he was simply tired of living in the mountains.

of parked cars and power lines, a few blocks from a Walmart. There was a gated garage and a large olive tree obscuring its facade.

The hard part was waiting for the kingpin to arrive. Days, then weeks, went by and there was still no sign of movement in Los Mochis. Nor was there much to report from the mountains. With Chaneke at his side, Guzmán had apparently gone silent.

In early December, losing patience, the Marines decided to offer him encouragement. Dozens of troops, supported in the air by helicopter gunships, were sent up Highway 24 and started laying siege to La Tuna and the villages around it in an operation even more aggressive than the one that had been launched outside Cosalá. Roads were blocked, entire towns were overrun, Guzmán's brother's ranch was occupied and seized. The Sinaloans did not submit quietly to this. Bloody gunfights erupted in the streets and at least eight people were killed. But that was part of the strategy: to hit the kingpin hard, in his home, where it would hurt.

The Marines were sticking to their game plan. If he was going to hide up there living on tortillas, they were going to make damn sure he didn't get the luxury of beans.

Finally, near Christmas, there was chatter on the wire.

Orders from the boss to his underlings in Culiacán: He wanted them to pick up three bouquets of flowers and three new sets of sheets.

After all of it, was he really that predictable? It seemed he was.

With the holidays approaching, it appeared he was coming down to see his wives and girlfriends.[39]

___

39. From the testimony of Lucero Sánchez:
Q: How many times did you see him after he escaped from prison in 2015?
A: Twice.
Q: When were those times?
A: It was at the end of 2015 and the beginning of 2016. . . . I was with him for New Year's.

But how, the Marine commanders wondered, should they handle this new twist? Culiacán was a far better target than the mountains were but it was nowhere near as good a target as Los Mochis. It had to be possible to get him out of one and into the other.

A different plan, then: Do nothing.

It was the holidays, after all, and much of Mexico had already shut down. If the Marines shut down as well—pulled the troops from La Tuna, sent the undercovers in Los Mochis home—perhaps the kingpin would catch wind of it and decide to make a move.

Doing nothing was risky, and it relied on Guzmán still being tapped into the flow of rumor and military chitchat that moved through Mexico City. But once the Marines resolved to try it, they quietly spread the word.

The operation was going on a holiday hiatus.

Christmas in Mexico is generally celebrated from the Feast of the Virgin of Guadalupe to Three Kings Day, a period lasting from December 12 to January 6.

On January 7, one day after the season ended, Pegasus caught an interesting message.

Nana is coming, it said.

The undercovers, back in place, saw him arrive in Los Mochis.

A truck dropped him off within the city limits and a white van picked him up. Then the watchers—close behind the van—followed him to the white house in Las Palmas.

If they weren't sure at first that it was him, they were soon after. As midnight neared, one of his men hopped into the van and went to fetch supplies for the night: porn and an order of tacos.

*   *   *

The raid was set for early the following morning, January 8, 2016. There was no drone feed this time. Donovan got the details after it went down.

He was informed, as a preliminary matter, that seventeen Marines hit the safe house door at about four-thirty as dozens of support troops stayed outside to monitor the manhole covers up and down the block. He was also told that when the men on point stormed into the vestibule, they encountered what appeared to be a maze of walls and doorways. That was when they started taking fire.

Later he got the photographs: bodies slumped in corners or bleeding on the floor. The Marines advanced into the gunfire with hand grenades and rifles, sweeping through the house from room to room. They started in the kitchen, where junk food wrappers were strewn across the table, and moved toward the final bedroom, where a flat-screen TV set was playing on the wall.

By the time they left, five of Guzmán's men lay dead—among them his bodyguard Chaneke. But the kingpin himself was nowhere to be found. He had already fled with Cholo Ivan through La Quinta's latest invention.

Not the decoy tunnel underneath the fridge. The real one, hidden behind a mirror in the master bedroom closet.

Within hours, even the smallest regional papers had the rest of it.

Emerging from a manhole cover near the Walmart, Guzmán and Cholo Ivan stole a Volkswagen. When the Volkswagen stalled a few blocks later, they commandeered another car—a red Ford Focus—and took off south, headed out of town.

Some of the details varied, here and there: They had escaped with pistols or maybe an assault rifle; Cholo Ivan did, or perhaps did not, politely return a purse to the woman driving the Ford. It was, however, widely reported that when the federal police stopped their car at a checkpoint on the southbound lane of Highway 15, the officers who pulled them over were terrified. They had heard on their radios that an army of gunmen was already en route to rescue Guzmán. Hurrying their prisoners off the street, they took them, blocks away, to a quiet room in an hourly motel.

There, the police showed remarkable restraint in resisting every lever Guzmán tried to use on them, ignoring his death threats and turning down his offer of a million dollars.

Picking up a phone, they coolly placed a call to the Marines. Then waited, like heroes, for the cavalry to arrive.

And that was the end of it—except for one thing.

It was not at all what the coalition heard.

In the different story that had come to them from Mexico, no one had called the Marines to tell them that the kingpin had been captured. Instead, while chasing Guzmán somewhere near the city of Guasave, they drove by chance past a tow truck with a red Ford Focus on its lift.

The Marines immediately recognized the vehicle as the one that had been stolen, and after some persuasion, the tow truck driver confessed where he had gotten the car: from someplace called the Hotel Doux, on the outskirts of Los Mochis.

When the Marines raced over, they found two police officers hiding in the parking lot out back beside their squad car. In the car were Chapo Guzmán and Cholo Ivan Gastelum, their hands uncuffed, and apparently hiding too.

Were the men in the custody of the two courageous officers? Or were the officers in league with them?

And why had they been taken to an hourly motel and not to jail?

The coalition had its opinions.

But those were questions better left to the Mexican authorities to answer on their own.

ELEVEN

Second Coming

After three arrests, two escapes and more near misses than it cared to count, the United States government had finally had enough. Officials at the highest levels in Washington had come to a decision. Now that Guzmán was back in custody, them wanted him on American soil.

At least in theory they had a way of getting him there. Guzmán, by then, had been named in seven indictments in seven different judicial districts and all of them were solid cases, ready to take to court. In El Paso, prosecutors had gathered evidence that he was involved in unspeakable violence on the border. In Chicago, the Flores brothers and Vicente Zambada—backed up by the Crackberry wire—were prepared to take the stand. The trove of intercepts that Marston, Potash and Christian Rodriguez had collected had led to charges in Manhattan. Equally damning messages obtained in Nogales had been used to bolster preexisting complaints in Brooklyn and Miami. Even the little prosecutor's office in Concord, New Hampshire, had a case against the kingpin on its books.

First, however, someone had to get him out of Mexico, and that wasn't going to be easy. Extraditing criminals from the country was a tortuous and time-consuming process. Under Mexican law, defendants were allowed to file an almost endless series of *amparos*, or injunctions, submitting one in the capital and then, if it failed, in Chihuahua or Sonora, on and on, like a game of legal whack-a-mole. The one restraining factor in the process was how much money and how many lawyers a defendant had, and Guzmán had plenty of both.

The politics of the situation weren't much better. There were, of course, substantial benefits to sending Guzmán north across the border. In a single stroke, the Mexican government could wash its hands of a man who had chastened and embarrassed it for nearly thirty years. But the downsides to extradition were potentially catastrophic. No one knew what Guzmán, who was facing life in prison, might say to his American interrogators. If he chose to open up as part of a plea agreement or cooperation deal, his revelations about official corruption and complicity in the drug trade could easily have calamitous effects.

In the US embassy, a small team of officials led by the ambassador, Roberta Jacobson, was hurrying to get the process started. There were already concerns that Guzmán would attempt a third escape. The diplomats had been quietly chagrined when, after his recapture in Los Mochis, the kingpin was returned to Altiplano. The Mexican Interior Ministry, in full face-saving mode, had taken several steps to beef up security at the prison, increasing the number of its cameras, installing steel bars in the floors to protect against tunnels and posting tanks and troops outside the walls. Guzmán's guards had relieved him of the privilege of conjugal visits and had started to wake him at all hours of the night for spot inspections. But no one—or certainly no one at the embassy—had any real faith in the system.

"There was a very strong assumption that he was planning an escape," Ambassador Jacobson said. "And that was discussed with the Mexicans. We had to assume that none of the facilities he might be sent to were foolproof in their ability to hold him." Jacobson and her colleagues felt like they were fighting both the clock and the leisurely Mexican courts. "Unless we got things moving," she said, "we feared he might get out again."

At least Los Piños, the Mexican White House, was sending the proper signals. A few weeks after the capture in Los Mochis, President Peña Nieto, traveling in Davos, announced that he was planning to fast-track extradition. It was a promising turnaround from two years earlier when Mexican officials had coyly rejected an American request. Following the kingpin's last arrest in Mazatlán, Jesús Murillo, the attorney general, had said he would consider extradition at "the right time." That, his advisors later noted, would be in a few hundred years, only after Guzmán had been sent to jail for the eight separate Mexican cases he was facing.

With momentum moving against them, the kingpin's lawyers opened a new front in the battle. After filing their first round of injunctions, they launched an all-out publicity campaign.

Throughout the winter of 2016, they gave interviews to anyone who would listen, complaining that the staff at Altiplano was violating Guzmán's human rights. It was bad enough, they said, that the prisoner had been turned into a zombie after weeks of being woken by his guards; but it was even worse that they themselves were allowed to see their client only once a week and for little more than a half hour at a time. At a press conference outside Altiplano's gates, one of the lawyers wore a sweatshirt with Guzmán's photo on the front and an exclamatory slogan shouting "EXTRADITION NEVER!" The lawyer announced that he was going on a hunger strike and begged his fellow Mexicans to join him.

Placing extra pressure on the government, the kingpin's lead attorney, José Refugio Rodríguez, cleverly adopted the president's own position. He signaled that his client would welcome extradition—even plead guilty in the United States—under one suspicious condition. Refugio demanded that in exchange for Guzmán's cooperation, American officials had to agree not to send him to a maximum security prison. "Physically he's in very bad shape," Refugio said. "If they don't let him sleep, he'll die."

Adding a personal touch to all of this was Emma Coronel. In her nine years of marriage to the kingpin, Emma had maintained an aristocratic distance from the public, supporting her husband—and burnishing her own myth—through the mysteries of a calculated silence. But starting in February, one month after Guzmán's arrest, she began to dangle herself in a series of stage-managed, on-the-record interviews.

The first stop on her tour was Telemundo, the Spanish-language broadcasting giant, which heavily promoted her Sunday evening prime-time appearance as the first-ever conversation with "El Chapo's Queen." Dressed demurely in a sleeveless blouse with a white bow at her throat, Emma fed the network a string of casual lies. She told her interviewer that at least as far as she knew, her drug lord husband had never trafficked drugs. Nor, she insisted, had he had ever said "a bad word" or gotten "upset at anyone." In all of this, Emma drew a sharp distinction with Guzmán's jailers who, she complained without a trace of irony, were "watching him . . . all day long," stripping him of privacy even in the bathroom of his cell. Over the next few weeks, she repeated this performance two more times: first, for Univision, Telemundo's chief competitor, and then for the *Los Angeles Times*.

That same month, she paid a quiet visit to Damaso López.

When the chief of staff received her—in Culiacán, it seems—Emma brought regards from her husband and told Damaso a secret she had not revealed to her television audience. Guzmán was already planning his third escape.

It was "a huge effort," Emma said, and once again she asked for Damaso's help. Loyal to a fault, Damaso agreed to do what he could, though at a follow-up meeting he confessed to Emma that the Company's operations budget was running somewhat low. Still in place as the kingpin's regent, Damaso would have surely been aware of the troublesome developments that had slowly been eroding the cartel's profits. In 2012, the same year Guzmán was raided in Los Cabos, no less than three of his Colombian suppliers had been taken into custody, putting downward pressure on the Company's cocaine division. Much more recently, its marijuana business had been trending lower too, in part because of the move toward legalization in the state of California. Just before his last arrest, the kingpin had managed to recoup some of his losses by finding new sources of cocaine and astutely investing in experimental products like synthetic heroin. But with an expensive new escape plot in the offing, at least some part of Damaso's thoughts must have been focused on the effects it would have on the Company's bottom line.

Emma dismissed these worries out of hand. Meeting Damaso for a third time, she arrived with money—or rather, with the promise of money: a hundred thousand dollars that had, she said, been earmarked for the purchase of another piece of land near Altiplano. As Damaso realized, the new escape plan wasn't new at all; it was merely a reprisal of the old plan.

Whatever it was, it soon hit a wall. In early May, after only four months at Altiplano, Guzmán was rousted from his cell one night and flown without warning to Ciudad Juárez, where he was imprisoned in a new facility: the shabby, gang-infested Cefereso No. 9. Not long after he arrived, his lawyers brought him more bad news: two judges had just denied their package of injunctions and approved his extradition to either San Diego or El Paso. The governments on both sides of the border seemed to be serious this time. The American requests for extradition had been sent to Mexico City in two separate dossiers. Both were nearly five inches thick.

Trying desperately to keep their plan on track, Emma reached out to Damaso one last time. She reassured him that Guzmán was working day and night to get out of Juárez and back to Altiplano, noting that her husband had already sent a generous gift to an official who could make that happen: one of the top men in the Mexican prison system. When Damaso asked her how much had been spent on the gift, he could not have been pleased by the answer.

"I was told," he later said, "it was two million dollars."

Daunting as it was, and it must have seemed impossible, if anyone was up to the job of keeping the Company running, it was certainly Damaso. For almost two decades, he had been the rock at the center of the empire: the one man who could be counted on completely to move the boss's merchandise, solve his problems and guard his darkest secrets.

As his nickname—El Licenciado[40]—suggested, Damaso was a different breed from the tough, unschooled Culichis who typically surrounded Guzmán. Born in El Dorado, a village south of Culiacán, he had been sent to law school by his father, a prominent local lawyer with connections to the PRI, and earned his first job in the state's public prosecutor's office through a recommendation from one of his professors. Damaso later went to work for the judicial state police, serving, ironically, on an antiviolence task force, and eventually landed at Puente Grande prison where he met the inmate Guzmán. When the kingpin broke out of Puente Grande, Damaso was initially

---

40. The title, which literally means the Licensed One, is an honorific bestowed on those who hold advanced degrees.

blamed for the escape. Embroiled in scandal and all but unemploy-able, he went to visit his onetime charge at one of his mountain lairs near Nayarit. A job was offered almost instantly. The disgraced for-mer official was asked to join the Company as a superintendent and real-estate agent, responsible for purchasing and managing the prop-erties the kingpin used for business. While his early pay was modest—fifteen hundred dollars a month—his potential for advancement was tremendous. Never lacking in ambition or intelligence, Damaso was quickly promoted to dealing with the kingpin's Colombian suppliers and soon took control of his New York distribution routes. Within a few years, Guzmán could barely make a deal or start a war without the former deputy warden at his side to give advice. "Damaso was a scary guy," a member of the coalition said. "He was just so slick and smart. If there was anyone to watch out for, it was him. Because you wouldn't see him coming."

Though Damaso was the obvious choice to run the kingpin's busi-ness, he himself was well aware that his promotion didn't sit well with the one group in the Company it most affected: his boss's four sons. Long before the succession plan was put in place, the *menores*—or "the young ones," as everybody called them—had resented and distrusted their father's chief of staff. After years of watching the boys' callow antics, Damaso distrusted them too. He had seen firsthand how Guz-mán's heirs—Iván, Alfredo, Ovidio and Joaquín—were little more than spoiled sons of privilege, forever squandering their patrimony on cheap women, expensive sports cars and exotic pets—interests that they documented obsessively on Instagram and Twitter. His own son, Damaso López Serrano, had at first run in their little brat pack—the so-called narco-juniors—and he had watched them all conducting busi-ness, signing their messages with smug millennial phrases ("Affirma-tive, bro . . .") and texting recklessly on the Company's communications system ("Drugs!!! . . . I need to work!!!") The older boys, Iván and Al-fredo, at least brought something that resembled revenue into the Company's coffers, working deals in Honduras and Los Angeles. Ovidio and Joaquín were hangers-on at best. They ran a few small meth labs in Culiacán and every now and then moved cocaine across the Arizona border. Occasionally, the younger sons were brought in as partners on large joint shipments, but it was mostly as a tribute to their father.

In the frantic days in 2014, when the Marines were preparing to stage their raid on Culiacán, Damaso had tried to have a talk with the boss about his boys. Iván and Alfredo had just escaped arrest while eating out in a restaurant, slipping away only after some waiters had helpfully changed clothes with them and snuck them out the door. Damaso wrote to Guzmán, boldly warning him that if the *menores* didn't strike a lower profile and keep away from "the mouths of women and assholes," the Company would suffer. The kingpin, while not quite disagreeing, seemed oddly tolerant of his prodigal sons.

> **11:34 P.M.:** There is nothing else to do but deal with children because they are our blood. . . . You have to be advising them, not scolding, because then it is worse.[41]

Blood or no blood, the closer that the kingpin moved toward extradition, the harder it became to keep his empire—and his family—together.

From the moment Guzmán returned to prison, Iván and Alfredo had been searching for a villain to blame. In a fit of filial vengeance,

---

41. To their credit, many of the narco-juniors did not come of age easily. Mayo Zambada's son, Serafin, testified at his sentencing hearing in San Diego in March 2018 that a car bomb had exploded outside his birthday party when he was two years old. Seven years later, he said, assassins stormed into a Mazatlán hotel room, killing his grandparents and his aunt and uncle. At his own sentencing hearing, in 2019, Serafin's older brother, Vicente, said that a hit squad tried to murder him—for the first time—when he was only sixteen.

they had first turned their attention toward the officers who had taken him into custody, sending out their loyalists to track down and identify the men. But according to Damaso, the focus of their suspicions soon began to change. In the end, they fell on someone who was much closer to home: their father's longtime partner, Mayo Zambada.

Not much had changed for Mayo himself after Guzmán's arrest. With typical judiciousness, he had decided to play a waiting game and took the middle road between embracing and distancing himself from Guzmán's sons. Mayo had always been exceptionally cautious: he often ate breakfast in one place, lunch in another and took his siesta in a third. At sixty-eight, Mayo had been working as a trafficker for more than fifty years and had in his seniority achieved the respect and admiration of an elder statesmen. While he generally thought of the *menores* as a nuisance, he knew that for the sake of peace within the Company, they had to be endured.

That spring, when Iván and Alfredo asked for an audience at El Alamo, his baronial estate in a Spanish-style compound outside Culiacán, Mayo, a paragon of ceremony, granted their request. When the boys arrived and expressed their concerns about their father, the wise old trafficker told them not to worry. He reassured them that the arrangements he had reached with Guzmán long ago still remained intact and that the family would continue to receive its regular portion of his profits. Whether these promises were genuine or not, Iván and Alfredo walked away from the encounter full of doubts. Within a few days, they went to see Damaso with an unthinkable proposal: they wanted to assassinate Zambada. Damaso claims that his first response was to ask the boys if they had spoken with their father and gotten his permission. When they admitted they had not, Damaso refused all further talk about the plot.

It is impossible to say exactly when the Company cracked open and splintered into separate warring factions, but by late in the spring of 2016 the fault lines were seething beneath the surface. Guzmán's federation had never been a cohesive organization. Even from its start, it had more resembled a medieval aristocracy than a chartered corporation, and was held together in good times by money and marital alliances, and was riven in bad times by brute displays of violence. But now with its profits under threat and one of its top warlords on the sidelines, the center couldn't hold. Fiefdoms started forming. Rebranding themselves as "Los Chapitos," Guzmán's sons claimed one corner of the kingdom and seized control of Culiacán. The kingpin's brother Aureliano claimed another piece from his base in Badiraguato, near La Tuna. Damaso, marshaling an army—Damaso's Special Forces—took a third slice, centered in El Dorado. Behind El Alamo's stuccoed walls, Mayo Zambada was somewhere in the middle, committing himself to no one and maintaining ties to everyone. But with his talent for deception, it was hard to tell if he was playing the role of an umpire or a vulture.

With its house divided, the Company soon had enemies at its gates. Only weeks after Guzmán's extradition was approved, a gang of as many as one hundred fifty gunmen descended on La Tuna. Entering the kingpin's village in a convoy of trucks and SUVs, the armed invaders moved past its modest shops and shacks, and snaked up into the hills toward the pillared ocher mansion where Guzmán's mother—who was nearly ninety—lived. There, inconceivably, they broke into the house, sacking its rooms and severing its phone lines. Reports came down from the mountains that when neighbors tried to protect Maria Loera, they were killed.

Two months later it happened again. This time, Alfredo, the kingpin's second son, was abducted at gunpoint at a bachelor party at La Leche, a white-walled seafood bistro near the beach in Puerto Vallarta. Seven gunmen carrying assault rifles stormed into the dining room on a Monday night in August and forced the cartel scion and a half-dozen others to their knees. They were spirited away, and it took nearly a week of backroom negotiations before they were released.

The two attacks were far more than brazen and unprecedented signs of disrespect: they were watershed moments in the drug trade's geopolitics. Both of them were ultimately blamed on Alfredo Guzmán Beltran, the son of Alfredo Beltran-Leyva, who had, it seemed, waited patiently for more than eight years to exact revenge on Guzmán for his father's arrest. Even more troubling, the savvy upstart—who was one of the kingpin's nephews—had launched his assaults with the New Generation Jalisco Cartel, the Company's erstwhile partner in its wars against the Zetas, which was already making inroads on Sinaloa's plazas in Tijuana and Baja California.

Guzmán had for years made his living by spotting and exploiting the weaknesses of his rivals; now, in his own weak state, his rivals were doing it to him. But imprisoned in Juárez, he had no way of stopping the rebellion. The only tool at his disposal, the Company's upper management, was paralyzed by rumor and division. And it wasn't even clear that the Company's upper management still existed.

As a lame-duck king, there was little he could do but trust his lawyers and fight his extradition. But his lawyers weren't getting anywhere either.

All of their appeals had been rejected, and some were quite creative. They had complained that he was freezing in his cell, that the charges against him had legally expired and that his only human contact was with prison guards in ski masks. In a final failed attempt, they had even claimed that he would never get a fair trial in the United States. The environment up north, the lawyers said, was just too hostile toward Mexicans—because of Donald Trump.

By Christmas, the embassy was feeling optimistic. Only one court, the Fifth Collegiate Panel for Criminal Matters in the capital, had not yet considered Guzmán's case.

Nothing, of course, would happen until January 6, when the holidays were over, but the embassy was hearing it would now be weeks, not months. Ambassador Jacobson and the rest of her team were not quite ready to celebrate, but they were getting close.

They had made their decision.

"It was only after he was back in the United States awaiting arraignment," the ambassador said, "that we were going to get some good tequila and finally have a drink."

It wasn't weeks—it was days.

On January 19, 2017, the Fifth Collegiate Panel in Mexico City rejected the last appeal. That same evening, at about five-thirty, Chapo Guzmán was taken from his cell in Juárez and, smelling of the prison where he had been for months, was placed in handcuffs and put on a police jet. No one told him where he was going. Even his own lawyers didn't know he was on board.

With him on the plane were three officials from the Mexican government and two American law enforcement agents. For more than four hours, as the plane veered east then north, the Americans said nothing. No introductions. No light small talk. Not a word.

It was only when the plane began descending in the darkness toward an unfamiliar airport—MacArthur Airport on Long Island—that Guzmán turned in confusion to his countrymen and asked where they were taking him.

One of the Americans finally spoke to him—in Spanish.

"Welcome," he said, "to the United States."

United States v. Guzmán

The American criminal justice system isn't known for its vibrant sense of irony, but it came up with a good one on January 20, 2017, just in time for Donald Trump's inauguration. On the same day, at practically the same hour, that much of the country watched the swearing in of a man who had launched his political career by attacking bad *hombres* coming in from Mexico, Mexico's worst *hombre*—the drug lord Joaquín Guzmán Loera—made his first appearance in federal court.

Like most things in the drug war, it was impossible to know from the perspective of the moment if this coincidence of timing was coincidental or was instead a surreptitious effort to upstage Trump with a theatrical distraction. After all, if anyone could compete with the headline-hungry president for attention, it was Chapo Guzmán. Like Trump himself, Chapo had been a single-name celebrity for decades; he, too, had earned a massive fortune during his career—and the kingpin's billions at least had the benefit of being verifiable. While both men had long been creatures of the media and styled themselves as simple, rough-hewn leaders, it was only after Trump's election that he acquired the concrete means of enforcing his will on life in the United States. Through endless acts of violence and corruption, Guzmán by that point had been shaping events in Mexico for nearly thirty years.

Certainly to those of us who spent Inauguration Day at the Brooklyn federal courthouse, the kingpin's arraignment in the early afternoon didn't feel like a second-rate assignment. With the kind of protection typically reserved for heads of state, Guzmán had arrived that morning from his jail cell in Manhattan in a traffic-stopping convoy of a dozen government vehicles. First had come the police vans with dome lights flashing, then an imposing row of unmarked SUVs. Only after the full parade had passed through a checkpoint near the court's garage had the prisoner himself appeared—in an armored car followed by an ambulance. Waiting for him inside the courthouse, there was more: federal agents with semiautomatics were stationed in the lobby; bomb-sniffing dogs were on patrol in the hallways; and a two-man team of US marshals—with little wands and backpack sensors—were inspecting all the garbage cans for ambient radiation.

As dozens of us packed into the courtroom, we were eager to see how the captured kingpin would react to all of this. Hours earlier, the Justice Department had issued a triumphant statement announcing the proceeding in which it had referred to Guzmán as "one of the principal leaders of the Sinaloa Cartel"—an accurate description that nonetheless left unsaid almost everything that mattered about the man. Whatever else he was, Chapo Guzmán was no mere cartel boss; by almost any standard, he was one of the top ten criminals in history. In the course of thirty years, he had smuggled nearly a million kilograms of drugs across the border—and that was just the fraction that the authorities had known about or seized. His wars of conquest and fits of vengeance had led to untold casualties in Mexico and helped to plunge his country into its bloodiest era since the Mexican Revolution. Throughout it all, he had remained an outlaw hero on a par with Al Capone and Jesse James, a folklore figure revered in songs and snuff films. Waiting for him to be hauled in from his holding cell, we expected someone worthy of the legend: Houdini, Zorro and Escobar all rolled up in one.

When he was finally brought in, he was nothing of the sort. A side door opened in the spacious room and out walked a man in a pair of blue pajamas. Even prepared by his famous nickname—"Shorty"—we saw at once that Guzmán was shrunken and diminished: a full foot smaller than the hulking guards who put him in front of the judge. With his sunken cheeks and jailhouse pallor, the kingpin looked confused, turning over his shoulder more than once to stare at the rows of faces staring back at him. He didn't look at all like a mythic criminal mastermind. Blinking in the bright fluorescent lights, he looked like a man who made his living selling snack food on the subway.

It started with a question.

"Are you Mr. Guzmán?" the judge inquired.

"*Sí, señor,*" he said.

Do you understand you have a right to an attorney?

"*Sí, señor,*" he said.

Have you reviewed the charges you are facing?

"*Sí, señor,*" he said.

Do you understand those charges?

"Well," the fabled drug lord answered, "I didn't . . . until now."

It was like that for months.

Whenever he showed up in court, he was a cipher: silent, vacant and drifting in what seemed to be a medicated daze. He rarely said a word, barely made a gesture and betrayed no sign of his celebrated wiliness or fortitude. Sitting at a table, in a foreign country, miles from his money and his empire, it appeared he had decided to simply get it over with and suffer through his fate. In the nearly two years that preceded his trial, his teams of lawyers—first a pair of public defenders, then a trio of retained attorneys—had done what they could for him, which wasn't all that much.

Starting at the end of the process, the lawyers attacked his extradition first. Officials in Mexico had initially consented to Guzmán being tried along the border—in either San Diego or El Paso—and the lawyers argued that by sending him to Brooklyn, they had broken their agreement. In a concurrent move that might have pleased their client, but had nothing to do with his multi-count indictment, they also complained about the kingpin's harsh conditions of confinement.

From the moment Guzmán arrived in New York, he was placed inside the one facility that was thought to be robust enough to hold him: Ten South, the dismal high-security wing of Manhattan's federal jail. In his solitary cell downtown, he was blasted by air-conditioning and monitored by cameras. His lights stayed on all night and his meals were passed to him through a slot in the door. On weekdays, he was given an hour of exercise on a treadmill and a stationary bike, but on Saturdays and Sundays he was caged around the clock. His only human contact came from his jailers: even his legal teams were forced to meet with him in separate rooms divided by a Plexiglas window. His letters were read, his phone calls were recorded, and the clock he purchased from the commissary was removed from him at one point without an explanation. With no view of the outside world, he could not tell time or distinguish day from night. After months of living in this limbo, Guzmán began to suffer headaches and had difficulty breathing. He claimed he was having aural hallucinations, hearing music when there wasn't any there.

Neither of these early issues was decided in his favor by the presiding judge in the case, Brian M. Cogan, a George W. Bush appointee who ultimately turned down nearly every one of the defense's requests. Those grew to include a motion to limit evidence about the kingpin's prior jailbreaks and an effort to suppress the cell-phone calls and FlexiSPY chats that the FBI and Christian Rodriguez had collected. As the trial date neared and their setbacks started mounting, Guzmán's lawyers took a final tack and asked for a delay in the proceedings. They argued that the government had dragged its feet during discovery and had, as a tactical matter, buried them in thousands of pages of complicated documents. In all of their maneuverings, however, none of the lawyers went so far as to argue that the kingpin wasn't guilty. The problem was that everybody knew he was guilty. On certain days, if they were in the proper frame of mind, the lawyers would acknowledge it themselves.

As the squabbling continued and the hearings dragged on, I made my own decision: I wasn't going to attend the trial itself. I had, by that point, been covering the courts for nearly twenty years and after sitting through murder trials, Mafia trials, terrorism trials and police corruption trials, I was confident that Chapo Guzmán's trial was going to be tedious at best. What else, I imagined, could still be said about a man who had lived in the spotlight since the early 1990s and had been picked apart by countless writers in countless books and news reports—not to mention a Netflix series, with a second on the way?

From the outset of the case, the public filings had been filled with facts that we already knew from the biographies and magazines: Guzmán had stashed his cocaine in cans of jalapeños and had once built a tunnel hidden beneath a pool table. In the first ten months of the prosecution, there was only one new story, as far as I could tell—a local traffic story. Every time the kingpin's motorcade took him to court, crossing the river from Manhattan into Brooklyn, the police department, fearing an escape, closed the Brooklyn Bridge.

In the end, however, the opportunity was just too big to miss, and feeling something like a hostile witness, I made my way to the Eastern District courthouse at six a.m. on November 13, 2018, the first day of the trial. Even at that early hour, an unruly line of dozens of reporters—from Bogotá, Caracas, Culiacán, Washington, Los Angeles, Chicago—was queued up on the sidewalk waiting to get in out of the freezing autumn dark. The federal building, in Brooklyn Heights, had seen its share of celebrity defendants, but the preparations and the appetite for this one were unprecedented. Quaint Cadman Plaza, once the province of family dogs and soccer moms, had been cut off from its neighborhood by what seemed like half the borough's squad cars and was under the watchful eye of an occupying army of body-armored riflemen. As I went inside the courthouse I stepped on the elevator with a team of black-clad snipers. Long guns at their shoulders, they were headed upstairs to take up their positions on the roof.

From the moment of its opening call—*United States v. Guzmán*—the trial erupted like a geyser and didn't stop for months.

Among the surprises that first day was one that was worth the wait: the kingpin was offering an actual defense. In his opening statement, Jeffrey Lichtman, Guzmán's most vivacious lawyer, spun a tale of deep-state conspiracy that seemed to have been plucked from an airport thriller novel.

Chapo Guzmán, Lichtman assured us, was not the real leader of the Sinaloa drug cartel, but was merely a convenient public scapegoat. The real leader was none other than his longtime partner, Mayo Zambada, who, we were informed, had orchestrated Guzmán's arrest with a corrupt cabal of Mexican presidents and crooked American cops. The myth of El Chapo, Lichtman said—the prison breaks, the border tunnels, the cinematic scenes in the Sierras—was precisely that: a myth. And the truth was disguised behind a veil of lies that obscured almost everything we knew about the drug war. Guzmán hadn't broken out of prison years ago simply to be free; he had broken out to evade the hired assassins scheming to eliminate him. He hadn't fled to the mountains hiding from the army or the CIA; he had fled to save his life. For more than two decades, Lichtman said, Guzmán had either been in custody or on the run from the authorities, who had hunted him like an animal. Under such conditions, how could he have possibly built a multibillion-dollar empire with hundreds of underlings on four different continents? The answer was he hadn't— Mayo Zambada had. The same Mayo Zambada, Lichtman reminded us, who had smuggled drugs for more than four decades, but never spent a single night in jail.

In terms of pure intrigue, this was good material—not the least because even Lichtman's most implausible allegations were adjacent to the facts. Guzmán really had been locked in prison or running from the authorities for most of his career. Mayo Zambada really hadn't been arrested in all that time despite the fact that many of his allies, enemies and children had either wound up dead or in custody themselves. The Mexican government, it hardly needed saying, really was corrupt.

By the end of that first week, the lackluster trial I had expected had turned into a kind of narco-opera—something like what might have resulted if Wagner, García Márquez and Elmore Leonard had all gone down to Tijuana to write the book and music with a case of Centenario. At the heart of the performance was the star-studded cast. Never before had prosecutors at a Mexican drug trial brought together so many witnesses from inside a cartel. Every other morning, another one of Guzmán's friends or colleagues stepped onto the courtroom's stage and mesmerized the audience with arias about the kingpin shipping cocaine in trucks of live sheep or jetting off to Switzerland for rejuvenation cures. The witnesses' own stories were equally remarkable, filled with accounts of cartel swag caps and of murders attempted with poisoned cornmeal pastries. It all began with Mayo's brother Rey, who offered a master class in the organization's history and macroeconomics, and ended twelve weeks later with Memin Valdez, Guzmán's former gunman, who spoke of locking his victims into cowsheds and searing them with clothing irons. In between, like the ghosts in *A Christmas Carol*, there were turns on the stand by Miguel

Angel Martínez, the kingpin's first employee; Juan Carlos Ramírez, his Colombian supplier; Pedro Flores, his American distributor; and a host of other by now familiar faces: Vicente Zambada, Damaso López, the two Cifuentes brothers, Christian Rodriguez and the luckless mistress Lucero Sánchez.

Some of their testimony covered old ground. It had long been known that Guzmán acquired his drugs from South and Central America in an ever-changing fleet of speedboats, submarines and single-engine Cessnas, then moved it north across the border in tanker trains of cooking oil equipped with secret compartments and in crates of meat in the backs of eighteen-wheelers. It was also not a new revelation that over the years his billion-dollar fortune had compromised almost every level of the government in Mexico, from mayors to generals—some said even presidents—and supported a payroll of pilots, drivers, accountants, gunsmiths, couriers and lawyers, along with the lookouts posted throughout the country who spied on his behalf.

But what nobody had heard or seen before were the firsthand accounts of any of this—or the real human beings who had done these things themselves. Their presence in the courtroom breathed fresh life into the stale old tales and resulted in some new ones. From a narrative perspective, this was stunning. It was almost inconceivable that a man who had been probed and plumbed by journalists since 1993 had so much left to give.

Halfway through the trial, something happened. After almost two years of aphasia, Guzmán suddenly came to life.

Until that point, the only discernible emotions he had showed were toward his wife. Emma Coronel was a fixture in the courtroom, showing up each day in the latest cartel fashions, usually accompanied by lawyers, publicity agents and a heavy cloud of Poison by Dior.

On many mornings, as the guards brought Guzmán into court, he would rise up on his tiptoes, find her in the crowd and offer her a loving little wave. As he started to awaken, he seemed unable to resist trading similar gestures with the witnesses. When Alex Cifuentes took the stand, he glanced across the room at his old boss and gave a solemn nod that seemed like both a greeting and a kind of apology. Guzmán nodded back, as if to say "It's fine, my friend. Relax. This is how it always had to end."

The case, by then, was careening toward its preordained conviction. But even though the prosecution's evidence was overwhelming and the threat of life in prison was increasingly inevitable, Guzmán was becoming more expansive. Now, each day, he was furiously scribbling on a legal pad and greeting his lawyers with cheerful hugs and handshakes every time he saw them. It could have simply been that after twenty months in solitary confinement he had once again found pleasure in community—even if the community he had found was largely there to watch his guilty verdict. It could, of course, have also been that with nothing left to lose and with all eyes trained on him, he was starting to enjoy himself.

None of us could really understand him. His world was a mad world, after all, a hallucinatory whirl of secret hideouts, mountaintop airstrips, diamond-studded pistols, teenage prostitutes, encrypted cell phones, rubber-banded money and airplanes set on fire in the middle of the jungle. The central subjects of his trial—murder, drugs, corruption—were among the most serious that one could imagine and yet they were presented in an atmosphere of unrelieved insanity. The more Guzmán revealed himself, the more it was obvious that these two poles—absurdity and gravity, the idiot and the mastermind—were the basic architecture that formed his personality. There wasn't any separating one from the other.

It could have been predicted that he would ultimately turn the trial into his own telenovela. On the day Lucero Sánchez appeared in court, she testified at length about her love affair with Guzmán, then ran off the witness stand after bursting into tears. Emma Coronel was sitting only thirty feet away, pretending to feel nothing and casually pulling at the split ends of her hair. The following day, she and Guzmán were back in court for the second half of his mistress's account wearing outfits that Emma had picked out for them: identical burgundy velvet smoking jackets. The message, while ridiculously delivered, was as pitiless as a horse's head in a mobster's bed. Lucero, the other woman, was an insignificant felon dressed in prison clothes. Emma and her husband, the royal couple, were in red.

And so it went, up until the final moment on February 12, 2019. When the jurors returned that day from their last deliberations, Guzmán received their verdict—guilty on all counts—with the strangely muted look of a man who had been told that the brakes he had installed on his car last month would now need re-replacing. He had been far more demonstrative on any number of other days in court, including the one on which Alejandro Edda, the actor who portrayed him on *Narcos: Mexico*, had come to see him on a reconnaissance mission. When Edda walked into the room that morning, one of Guzmán's lawyers quietly leaned over to inform him that the man who played him on TV was in the gallery. His face lit up with a beatific grin.

Though the trial had marked one of the most visible victories for US law enforcement since the war on drugs had started in the early 1970s, it did almost nothing to halt the flow of illegal narcotics from pouring across the border. On January 31, the same day closing arguments were held, border officials in Arizona made a startling announcement: They had just seized the largest load of fentanyl ever found in the United States. The haul, they said, had been hidden in a truck transporting cucumbers through the Nogales port of entry, a crossing that the Sinaloa drug cartel had run for years.

Many of us held out hope for something more decisive at the king-pin's sentencing that summer. While Guzmán had come close—very close—to testifying in his own defense, he had eventually been dis-sauded from the gambit by his lawyers, who no doubt noticed how eager the prosecution team had been to cross-examine him. By tradi-tion, defendants are given the opportunity to address the court when they are sentenced and Guzmán's sentencing, which was slated for July, was going to be his last chance to address anyone ever again. It was a virtual certainty that after his penalty was handed down, he would be sent to the Supermax, the country's most secure federal prison, in Florence, Colorado, where he would be locked in isolation for the remainder of his days. As his hearing approached, there was a quiet expectation that he might finally let loose, spilling all his secrets and naming various names.

The day of the sentencing had an air of homecoming about it. Victor Vazquez came up to Brooklyn from his new assignment in Peru. Fern Cruz flew in from his own new posting in Atlanta. Mar-ston and Potash, still in Lower Manhattan, got up early to be sure that Andrea Velez, who was planning to address the court herself, made it safely to and from the courthouse. Ray Donovan—now in charge of the DEA's office in New York—wanted to be there too, but something had come up with his wife. He had already given enough years of his life to Chapo Guzmán and agreed to be with her when she asked him, for once, to let it go.

After some preliminary business, Judge Cogan turned and looked down at the kingpin.

"All right, Mr. Guzmán," he began, "you have the right to be heard. Is there anything that you would like to say?"

"Yes, your honor," Guzmán answered. "Thank you very much."

For the next ten minutes, after blessing his wife, his family and all of those who had kept him in their prayers, Guzmán embarked on a diatribe about the deep unfairness of it all, complaining about his extradition, his three-month trial and his state of incarceration. He claimed that he was being tortured around the clock in his cell across the river, forced to drink unsanitary water, breathe old air and block his ears with toilet paper to drown out the noises of the ventilation system. Arriving in this country, he explained, he had expected to receive a fair trial from a system he had hoped would be blind to his fame and reputation. But that hadn't happened. There had been no fairness, he insisted, and no real justice; his case was stained, and the entire world was watching. What had happened here, he said, had convinced him of an unassailable fact: "The United States is not better than any other corrupt country . . . that you do not respect."

Certain human beings have the power to hold a gaze. Without even asking for it, they command our attention, the most valuable commodity we have. As petulant as all of this was, Guzmán had been right about one thing: the world had been watching him, much like it had always watched him, millions of people, across the planet, for nearly thirty years. The important questions—Why had it been watching? Did he deserve it? And what was the point of all that concentration?—never seemed to have occurred to him. Perhaps he took it for granted. Or perhaps he understood what we did not: that no matter what he did and no matter what he said—no matter what happened—all of us were going to look at him.

Note on Sources and Style

Any book on Chapo Guzmán is doomed to run into a frustrating series of reporting roadblocks—chief among them the fact that the Sinaloa drug cartel has no equivalent of the National Archives or the Federal Records Act. The organization's day-to-day business has always, by necessity, taken place in a netherworld of concealment and obscurity where inaccuracies—or just as bad, fairy tales—are likely to grow. To complicate matters, many people with direct personal knowledge of the cartel's operations lie beyond the reach of normal journalistic methods by virtue of their status as either fugitives from justice or federally protected cooperating witnesses. The efforts of the US government to investigate and prosecute syndicates like Guzmán's have themselves long been veiled by an almost impenetrable form of official secrecy. Thousands—perhaps even tens of thousands—of documents in scores of case files related to the kingpin and his colleagues remain under seal to this day. They contain what amounts to the untold history of the Mexican drug war.

That said, this book was put together from three primary sources: firsthand interviews with most of its central characters; the voluminous transcript from Guzmán's twelve-week trial; and thousands of pages of investigative records from both his and ancillary cases, many of which were brought into the public light for the first time.

Contemporaneous news reports on relevant events were used as well, albeit sparingly, given that initial accounts of events in the drug war have a vexing habit of changing over time. Javier Rey's biographical manuscript on Guzmán also proved helpful in fleshing out parts of the kingpin's early years.

Several sources who generously offered their time and insights could not be named or conclusively identified under the terms of agreements with the government. As a counterweight to the anonymity provided by these agreements, I developed a rule of thumb. Whenever it was possible, facts were confirmed by at least two, and often three or four, separate sources, as those who were pestered endlessly on weekends and holidays will know. On occasion, I included facts from a single source, but only from those who proved to be extraordinarily trustworthy. By contrast, if more than one unreliable source offered similar facts, their contributions were not included.

The narrative style in which this book is written sometimes required the use of the conditional tense to get past unknown and unknowable gaps in the story line or in its characters' internal lives. Those moments are clearly flagged for the reader by the presence of indicative phrases like "it seems" or "it must have been."

A final note: Even as I write, the story of Chapo Guzmán continues to unfold. There is a chance that with more time than the ten months it took to conceive, research, write and edit this book I could have more aggressively pursued the numerous Mexican officials who took part in the chase (nearly all of whom declined my attempts to speak with them) or gotten access to Guzmán's longtime enemy, Alfredo Beltran-Leyva, in prison. It might also have been possible to have fully told the story of how Ray Donovan found his way to the DEA after an early, aborted interest in becoming a pharmacist, or how Stephen Marston communicated by text with Andrea Velez while she was undercover in Mexico by pretending to be her boyfriend.

But, like the hunt for El Chapo himself, the hunt for his story in its entirety will no doubt be a long and arduous one. Secret documents I have sought to unseal are even now still being released and evidence of the CIA's role in the chase may never be completely revealed. If I know one thing for certain, however, it is that the tale of the man notorious for evading capture will not be caught easily; more information will undoubtedly come to light in the months and years going forward. With that in mind, I can only hope that this book will serve as a guidepost and resource for the next author who approaches the subject and picks up these threads to continue the work.

Acknowledgments

Writing this book would not have been possible without the generous assistance of several people. Great thanks are due to Will Murphy, who stepped in at the last minute as an editor, and to Lauren Bittrich at Flatiron Books, who skillfully helped to shape the final manuscript. I owe an even larger debt to my agent, David Halpern, who guided me with a steady hand through the many excitements and emergencies of the writing process.

I would also like to thank Erin McKenzie-Mulvey at the DEA, Angela Bell at the FBI and Yasmeen Pitts O'Keefe at HSI for their invaluable help in arranging interviews with their investigators. While many of those people cannot be named here, they know who they are.

Finally, all of my love and gratitude to my wife, Joanna, for her great support, endless patience and inexhaustible good spirits during the sprinted marathon of making this book. She is, and always has been, The Best.

About the Author

ALAN FEUER covers courts and criminal justice for the Metro desk at *The New York Times*. He has written about mobsters, jails, police misconduct, wrongful convictions, and government corruption. He lives in New York City.